TO

_____

FROM

_____

DATE

_____

FAMILY
CHRISTIAN
PRESS

30 Lessons from The Life of David

Dr. Criswell Freeman

Copyright ©2006 Family Christian Press

The quoted ideas expressed in this book (but not scripture verses) are not, in all cases, exact quotations, as some have been edited for clarity and brevity. In all cases, the author has attempted to maintain the speaker's original intent. In some cases, quoted material for this book was obtained from secondary sources, primarily print media. While every effort was made to ensure the accuracy of these sources, the accuracy cannot be guaranteed. For additions, deletions, corrections or clarifications in future editions of this text, please write FAMILY CHRISTIAN PRESS.

Scripture quotations are taken from:

The Holy Bible, King James Version

The Holy Bible, New International Version (NIV) Copyright © 1973, 1978, 1984, by International Bible Society. Used by permission of Zondervan Publishing House. All rights reserved.

The New American Standard Bible®, (NASB) Copyright © 1960, 1962, 1963, 1968, 1971, 1972, 1973, 1975, 1977, 1995 by The Lockman Foundation. Used by permission.

The Holy Bible, New King James Version (NKJV) Copyright © 1982 by Thomas Nelson, Inc. Used by permission.

The Holy Bible, New Living Translation, (NLT) Copyright © 1996. Used by permission of Tyndale House Publishers, Inc., Wheaton, Illinois 60189. All rights reserved.

New Century Version®. (NCV) Copyright © 1987, 1988, 1991 by Word Publishing, a division of Thomas Nelson, Inc. All rights reserved. Used by permission.

The Holy Bible: Revised Standard Version (RSV). Copyright 1946, 1952, 1959, 1973 by the Division of Christian Education of the National Council of the Churches of Christ in the United States of America. All rights reserved. Used by permission.

The Holy Bible, The Living Bible (TLB), Copyright © 1971 owned by assignment by Illinois Regional Bank N.A. (as trustee). Used by permission of Tyndale House Publishers, Inc., Wheaton, Illinois 60189. All rights reserved.

The Message (MSG) This edition issued by contractual arrangement with NavPress, a division of The Navigators, U.S.A. Originally published by NavPress in English as THE MESSAGE: The Bible in Contemporary Language copyright 2002-2003 by Eugene Peterson. All rights reserved.

The Holman Christian Standard Bible™ (HOLMAN CSB) Copyright © 1999, 2000, 2001 by Holman Bible Publishers. Used by permission.

Cover Design by Kim Russell / Wahoo Designs
Page Layout by Bart Dawson

ISBN 1-58334-372-5

Printed in the United States of America

30 Lessons from The Life of David

Dr. Criswell Freeman

TABLE OF CONTENTS

INTRODUCTION

Even if you have only a passing acquaintance with the Bible, you're familiar with David, one of the pivotal figures in the Old Testament. Since the days of your childhood, you've heard David's name on countless occasions—but even if you've been a Christian for many years, you may not know too much about David's life or the lessons he was trying to teach. If so, this book contains powerful ideas that can revolutionize your day and your life.

God's Word is not a distant document designed only for the people of Old Testament times; it is a living document intended for you. And David's life—a dramatic tale of faith, obedience, and deliverance—is intended to serve as a powerful example for believers of every generation, including yours.

So, during the next 30 days, try this experiment: read one chapter a day and take the ideas in that chapter to heart. Then, apply those lessons to the everyday realities of your life. When you weave God's message into the fabric of your day, you'll quickly discover that God's Word has the power to change everything, including you.

KEY EVENTS IN THE LIFE OF DAVID

The Lord chooses David to be king
1 Samuel 16:1-13

David plays the harp for king Saul
1 Samuel 16:14-23

David kills Goliath
1 Samuel 17:1-54

Saul becomes jealous of David
1 Samuel 18:6-30

David's marriage to Saul's daughter Michal
1 Samuel 18:20-28; 19:9-17; 2 Samuel 6:20-23

David's friendship with Jonathan
1 Samuel 18:1-4; 20:1-42; 23:14-18; 2 Samuel 1:1-27

David meets and marries Abigail
2 Samuel 25:1-44

David becomes king of Judah
2 Samuel 2:1-7

David becomes king of Israel
2 Samuel 5:1-5; 1 Chronicles 11:1-3

David captures Jerusalem
2 Samuel 5:6-12; 1 Chronicles 11:4-9; 14:1-2

David brings the sacred chest to Jerusalem
2 Samuel 6:1-19; 1 Chronicles 13:1-14; 15:1-16:3

David and Bathsheba
2 Samuel 11:1-12:25

Solomon is born
2 Samuel 12:24-25

Absalom rebels against his father David
2 Samuel 15:1-12

Absalom dies and David mourns
2 Samuel 18:7-19:8

David counts the people
2 Samuel 24:1-25

David gives instructions to his son Solomon
1 Kings 2:1-9

David dies
1 Kings 2:10-12

Source: The American Bible Society

A BRIEF HISTORY
OF THE LIFE OF DAVID

David, the great king of Israel and one of the pivotal figures in the Old Testament, was the eighth and youngest son of Jesse of Bethlehem. Although the exact date of David's birth remains in question, some scholars estimate that date at or about 1040 B.C.

During his remarkable life, David was a shepherd, a musician, a poet, a giant-slayer, a soldier, and a king. And he was an ancestor of Joseph, the husband of Mary the mother of Jesus.

As a young man, David was fearless. While protecting his father's sheep, he killed both a lion and a bear using only a handheld club. Also, while tending his sheep, David became an accomplished harp player. So, when Saul, the king of the Israelites desired a harp-player for his court, his attendants recommended David who came to Saul and entered into his service. Saul became very fond of David, but in time, David returned to the relative anonymity of Bethlehem . . . but he would not remain in Bethlehem for long.

A few miles from Bethlehem, the Philistines and Israelites were waging battle in the valley of Elah. And so it was that David's father sent his youngest son to carry provisions for David's three older brothers, all of whom were fighting with King Saul. Upon his arrival at the camp of Israel, David could not help but observe the Philistine giant Goliath standing almost nine feet tall and bedecked in heavy bronze armor, Goliath had already challenged any Israelite to fight him "to the death." With the approval of Saul, David gladly volunteered to fight Goliath. As the giant taunted his younger foe, David picked up a stone, took out his sling, aimed, and launched a stone that struck Goliath's forehead and knocked him senseless. David then ran to the giant and killed him with Goliath's own sword. Thus, with a stone and a sling, David had, in a single stroke, felled the giant and routed the Philistines.

David's instant notoriety—and his popularity with the Israelites—made Saul jealous, so Saul plotted to kill David. All such plots were unsuccessful, and David even developed a deep friendship with Saul's son Jonathan.

Eventually, in order to escape the king's wrath, David fled King Saul and became a fugitive. After Saul's death, David became king of Judah, and then, within a few years, he was made king over all of Israel. After a series of military victories, David led his people in the capturing of Jerusalem, which he made his nation's religious capital.

David was an imminently successful man, but certainly not a sinless one. Perhaps his most notable transgression was his adultery with Bathsheba and the subsequent arranged murder of her husband Uriah. Yet David was also able to seek God's forgiveness, and he never took God's forgiveness lightly.

David's life remains one of the most remarkable histories recorded in the Old Testament. He slew Goliath; he defeated the Philistines; he captured Jerusalem; he even wrote 73 Psalms. And after naming his son Solomon as his successor, David died:

Then David rested with his fathers and was buried in the City of David. He had reigned forty years over Israel—seven years in Hebron and thirty-three in Jerusalem. So Solomon sat on the throne of his father David, and his rule was firmly established.

1 Kings 2:10-12 NIV

LESSON 1

GOD WORKS MIRACLES

Then David put his hand in his bag and took out a stone;
and he slung it and struck the Philistine in his forehead,
so that the stone sank into his forehead,
and he fell on his face to the earth.

1 Samuel 17:49 NKJV

The Message

As he prepared to meet Goliath, David armed himself with a slingshot and a few stones. David needed strength, courage, and a miracle. God provided all three.

Are you facing a very difficult situation? If so, remember that God took young David—a boy who possessed self-confidence and faith—and gave that boy everything he needed to slay a towering giant.

What giants are you facing today? And do you believe that God will help you conquer them? Hopefully so, because the very same God who helped David is ready, willing, and perfectly able to help you perform a miracle, too.

Sometimes, because we are imperfect human beings with limited understanding and limited faith, we place limitations on God. But, God's power has no limitations. God will work miracles in our lives if we trust Him with everything we have and everything we are. When we do, we experience the miraculous results of His endless love and His awesome power.

> Only God can move mountains, but faith and prayer can move God.
>
> E. M. Bounds

Miracles, both great and small, are an integral part of everyday life, but usually, we are too busy or too cynical to notice God's handiwork. We don't expect to see miracles, so we simply overlook them.

Do you lack the faith that God can work miracles in your own life? If so, it's time to reconsider. If you have allowed yourself to become a "doubting Thomas," you are attempting to place limitations on a God who has none. Instead of doubting your Heavenly Father, you must trust Him. Then, you must wait and watch . . . because something miraculous is going to happen to you, and it might just happen today.

A LESSON TO THINK ABOUT

God is in the business of doing miraculous things. You should never be afraid to ask Him for a miracle.

WHAT GOD'S WORD SAYS ABOUT MIRACLES

Looking at them, Jesus said, "With men it is impossible, but not with God, because all things are possible with God."

Mark 10:27 Holman CSB

But as it is written: "Eye has not seen, nor ear heard, nor have entered into the heart of man the things which God has prepared for those who love Him."

1 Corinthians 2:9 NKJV

I assure you: The one who believes in Me will also do the works that I do. And he will do even greater works than these, because I am going to the Father.

John 14:12 Holman CSB

For nothing will be impossible with God.

Luke 1:37 Holman CSB

You are the God who works wonders; You revealed Your strength among the peoples.

Psalm 77:14 Holman CSB

WORDS OF WISDOM ABOUT
MIRACLES

The impossible is exactly what God does.

Oswald Chambers

The most profane word we use is "hopeless." When you say a situation or person is hopeless, you are slamming the door in the face of God.

Kathy Troccoli

The miracles in fact are a retelling in small letters of the very same story which is written across the whole world in letters too large for some of us to see.

C. S. Lewis

I could go through this day oblivious to the miracles all around me or I could tune in and "enjoy."

Gloria Gaither

Notes to Yourself: _____

_____

_____

_____

_____

_____

_____

_____

_____

_____

_____

_____

_____

As you consider the things you've written in the space above, ask yourself these questions:

Do I believe that God can do miraculous things?

Do I remain watchful for miracles both large and small?

Do I believe that all things are possible for those who believe, or am I living under a cloud of pessimism and doubt?

LESSON 2

FRIENDS MATTER

Now when he had finished speaking to Saul,
the soul of Jonathan was knit to the soul of David,
and Jonathan loved him as his own soul. Saul took him that day,
and would not let him go home to his father's house anymore.
Then Jonathan and David made a covenant,
because he loved him as his own soul.

1 Samuel 18:1-3 NKJV

The Message

David and Jonathan were true soul mates who demonstrated the importance and the power of friendship.

David and Jonathan were the closest of friends. Jonathan was always supportive of David, always loyal, never jealous. Even when Jonathan's father, King Saul, predicted that David would one day be king (in Jonathan's stead), Jonathan was not bitter. When Saul became disillusioned with David, Jonathan intervened on David's behalf. And Jonathan risked his own life for David on more than one occasion. And David, we can be sure, would have done the same for Jonathan had their situations been reversed.

Genuine friendships, like the bond between David and Jonathan, should be treasured and nourished. How? A great place to start is by observing the Golden Rule. As Christians, we are governed by that rule—we are commanded to treat others as we would wish to be treated if we stood in their shoes. And when we treat others with kindness, courtesy, loyalty, and respect, we can build friendships that can last a lifetime.

> *Don't you realize that all of you together are the temple of God and that the Spirit of God lives in you?*
>
> *1 Corinthians 3:16 NLT*

Throughout the Bible, we are reminded to love one another and care for one another. In other words, the Bible teaches us that the quality and duration of our friendships are directly and inexorably related to the way we choose to treat our friends. If we treat our friends well, our friendships endure—if we don't, our friendships won't last for long.

Do you want to have loyal friends? Then be one. Do you want others to love you? Then love them. Do you want to build relationships that endure? Then you must be willing to give the effort and to make the sacrifices that are required to make your relationships endure. When it comes to building friendships—close friendships like the bond between David and Jonathan—there are no shortcuts.

A LESSON TO THINK ABOUT

You need fellowship with men and women of faith. And your Christian friends need fellowship with you.

WHAT GOD'S WORD SAYS ABOUT FELLOWSHIP

You must get along with each other. You must learn to be considerate of one another, cultivating a life in common.

1 Corinthians 1:10 MSG

Don't become partners with those who reject God. How can you make a partnership out of right and wrong? That's not partnership; that's war. Is light best friends with dark?

2 Corinthians 6:14 MSG

He keeps us in step with each other. His very breath and blood flow through us, nourishing us so that we will grow up healthy in God, robust in love.

Ephesians 4:16 MSG

You can develop a healthy, robust community that lives right with God and enjoy its results only if you do the hard work of getting along with each other, treating each other with dignity and honor.

James 3:18 MSG

WORDS OF WISDOM ABOUT
FELLOWSHIP

The Bible knows nothing of solitary religion.

John Wesley

I hope you will find a few folks who walk with God to also walk with you through the seasons of your life.

John Eldredge

When you received Jesus Christ as your personal Lord and Savior, you began a relationship not only with Him but also with all other Christians.

Billy Graham

We were created for community, fashioned for fellowship, and formed for a family, and none of us can fulfill God's purposes by ourselves.

Rick Warren

When true believers are awed by the greatness of God and by the privilege of becoming His children, then they become sincerely motivated, effective evangelists.

Bill Hybels

Notes to Yourself: _____

_____

_____

_____

_____

_____

_____

_____

_____

_____

_____

_____

_____

As you consider the things you've written in the space above, ask yourself these questions:

Do I understand the need to be an active member of my fellowship?

Does my fellowship help me grow emotionally and spiritually?

Am I a builder of bridges inside my church and outside it?

BE KIND
TO ALL

*Now David said, "Is there still anyone who is left of
the house of Saul, that I may show him kindness for
Jonathan's sake?" . . . So Mephibosheth dwelt in Jerusalem,
for he ate continually at the king's table.
And he was lame in both his feet.*

2 Samuel 9:1,13 NKJV

The Message

David demonstrated compassion when he discovered that
Mephibosheth, the crippled son of Jonathan, has fallen
upon hard times in a distant land. David invited the boy
to return to Jerusalem and dwell in the palace.

David demonstrated his compassion in an unusual way. Most kings of David's era tried to kill the family members of their rivals. And Mephibosheth was the grandson of David's rival Saul. But instead of having Mephibosheth killed—or instead of leaving the young man to fend for himself in a distant land—David sent for Mephibosheth and made the young man a guest in David's court. Thus David fulfilled his promise to show kindness to Jonathan's descendants.

Compassion never goes out of style. God's Word commands us to be compassionate, generous servants to those who need our support. As believers, we have been richly blessed by our Creator. We, in turn, are called to share our gifts, our possessions, our testimonies, and our talents.

> Be so preoccupied with good will that you haven't room for ill will.
>
> *E. Stanley Jones*

Concentration camp survivor Corrie ten Boom correctly observed, "The measure of a life is not its duration but its donation." These words remind us that the quality of our lives is determined not by what we are able to take from others, but instead by what we are able to share with others.

When we examine the New Testament, we see that the thread of compassion is woven into the very fabric of Christ's teachings. In Matthew 25:40 Jesus warns, "Verily I say unto you, Inasmuch as ye have done it unto one of the least of these my brethren, ye have done it unto me" (KJV). So if we wish to be genuine disciples of Christ, we must be generous and kind. Our Savior expects no less from us, and He deserves no less. Yet in the busyness and confusion of daily life, it is easy to lose focus, and it is easy to become frustrated. We are imperfect human beings struggling to manage our lives as best we can, but we often fall short. When we are distracted or disappointed, we may neglect to share a kind word or a kind deed. This oversight hurts others, but it hurts us most of all.

Today, slow yourself down and be alert for those who need your smile, your kind words, or your helping hand. Make kindness a centerpiece of your dealings with others. They will be blessed, and you will be, too

A LESSON TO THINK ABOUT

Kindness is contagious. So make sure that your family and friends—and even strangers—catch it from you!

WHAT GOD'S WORD SAYS ABOUT KINDNESS

Be kind to each other, tenderhearted, forgiving one another, just as God through Christ has forgiven you.

Ephesians 4:32 NLT

Carry each other's burdens, and in this way you will fulfill the law of Christ.

Galatians 6:2 NIV

Finally, all of you should be of one mind, full of sympathy toward each other, loving one another with tender hearts and humble minds.

1 Peter 3:8 NLT

And may the Lord make you increase and abound in love to one another and to all.

1 Thessalonians 3:12 NKJV

So, as those who have been chosen of God, holy and beloved, put on a heart of compassion, kindness, humility, gentleness and patience.

Colossians 3:12 NASB

WORDS OF WISDOM ABOUT KINDNESS

Do all the good you can. By all the means you can. In all the ways you can. In all the places you can. At all the times you can. To all the people you can. As long as ever you can.

John Wesley

When you extend hospitality to others, you're not trying to impress people, you're trying to reflect God to them.

Max Lucado

It doesn't take monumental feats to make the world a better place. It can be as simple as letting someone go ahead of you in a grocery line.

Barbara Johnson

All kindness and good deeds, we must keep silent. The result will be an inner reservoir of personality power.

Catherine Marshall

Notes to Yourself: _____

_____

_____

_____

_____

_____

_____

_____

_____

_____

_____

_____

_____

_____

As you consider the things you've written in the space above, ask yourself these questions:

Do I look for situations where I can be helpful or courteous, or both?

Do I make kindness the cornerstone of my dealings with others?

Do I consistently treat other people in the same way that I want to be treated?

LESSON 4

RESIST
TEMPTATION

*Then it happened one evening that David arose from his bed
and walked on the roof of the king's house. And from the roof
he saw a woman bathing, and the woman was very beautiful to
behold. Then David sent messengers, and took her;
and she came to him, and he lay with her, for she was
cleansed from her impurity; and she returned to her house.*

2 Samuel 11:2-4 NKJV

The Message

When David saw Bathsheba, he succumbed to
temptation . . . and as a result, he committed adultery
which led, in turn, to murder.

When David saw Bathsheba, he fell prey to temptation; by committing adultery, David sinned against God. We, like David, must confront temptation. But unlike David, we must learn to defeat temptation before we find ourselves trapped by sin, not after.

Because our world is filled with temptations, we confront them at every turn. The devil, it seems, is working overtime and causing heartache in more places and in more ways than ever before. We, as Christians, must remain vigilant. Not only must we resist Satan when he confronts us, but we must also avoid those places where Satan can most easily tempt us. And, if we are to avoid the unending temptations of this world, we must arm ourselves with the Word of God.

> It is easier to stay out of temptation than to get out of it.
>
> *Rick Warren*

In a letter to believers, Peter offered a stern warning: "Be sober, be vigilant; because your adversary the devil walks about like a roaring lion, seeking whom he may devour" (1 Peter 5:8 NKJV). What was true in New Testament times is equally true in our own. Satan tempts his prey and then devours them. And in these dangerous times, the tools that Satan uses to destroy his prey are more numerous than ever before.

As believers we must beware. And, if we seek righteousness in our own lives, we must earnestly wrap ourselves in the protection of God's Holy Word.

After fasting forty days and nights in the desert, Jesus Himself was tempted by Satan. Christ used scripture to rebuke the devil (Matthew 4:1-11). We must do likewise. The Holy Bible provides us with a perfect blueprint for righteous living. If we consult that blueprint each day and follow its instructions carefully, we build our lives according to God's plan. And when we do, we are secure.

A LESSON TO THINK ABOUT

Because you live in a temptation-filled world, you must guard your eyes, your thoughts, and your heart—all day, every day.

WHAT GOD'S WORD SAYS ABOUT TEMPTATION

No temptation has overtaken you except what is common to humanity. God is faithful and He will not allow you to be tempted beyond what you are able, but with the temptation He will also provide a way of escape, so that you are able to bear it.

1 Corinthians 10:13 Holman CSB

For we do not have a High Priest who cannot sympathize with our weaknesses, but was in all points tempted as we are, yet without sin. Let us therefore come boldly to the throne of grace, that we may obtain mercy and find grace to help in time of need.

Hebrews 4:15-16 NKJV

Put on the whole armor of God, that you may be able to stand against the wiles of the devil.

Ephesians 6:11 NKJV

The Lord knows how to deliver the godly out of temptations.

2 Peter 2:9 NKJV

WORDS OF WISDOM ABOUT
TEMPTATION

The only power the devil has is in getting people to believe his lies. If they don't believe his lies, he is powerless to get his work done.

Stormie Omartian

In the worst temptations nothing can help us but faith that God's Son has put on flesh, sits at the right hand of the Father, and prays for us. There is no mightier comfort.

Martin Luther

Our Lord has given us an example of how to overcome the devil's temptations. When he was tempted in the wilderness, He defeated Satan every time by the use of the Bible.

Billy Graham

Since you are tempted without ceasing, pray without ceasing.

C. H. Spurgeon

Notes to Yourself: _____

_____

_____

_____

_____

_____

_____

_____

_____

_____

_____

_____

As you consider the things you've written in the space above, ask yourself these questions:

Am I fully aware that I live in a society brimming with temptations?

Do I avoid places where I might be tempted to disobey God?

Do I avoid people who might encourage me to compromise my beliefs or betray my conscience?

ONE SIN LEADS TO ANOTHER

And he wrote in the letter, saying,
"Set Uriah in the forefront of the hottest battle,
and retreat from him,
that he may be struck down and die."

2 Samuel 11:15 NKJV

The Message

David's adultery with Bathsheba eventually caused David to send Bathsheba's husband Uriah to be killed in battle. What had begun in adultery ended in murder.

The story of David and Bathsheba teaches us that one sin often leads to another. After David had committed adultery with Bathsheba, he plotted a second, even more devastating offense: he sent Bathsheba's husband Uriah to the front lines of battle with instructions that David's soldiers were to abandon the innocent man when the fighting became fierce. David's soldiers followed these instructions, and Uriah was killed.

When he was informed of Uriah's death, David was almost flippant (1 Samuel 11:25). Why? Because David's heart had been hardened by sin.

> For all have sinned
> and fall short of
> the glory of God.
> Romans 3:23 Holman CSB

We, like David, are creatures of free will; we may disobey God whenever we choose, but when we do so, we put ourselves in great peril. Disobedience invites disaster.

We cannot sin against God without consequence. We cannot live outside His will without injury. We cannot distance ourselves from God without hardening our hearts. And we cannot yield to the ever-tempting distractions of our world and, at the same time, enjoy God's peace.

Sometimes, in a futile attempt to justify our misdeeds, we make a distinction between "big" sins and "little" sins. Or we may harden our hearts and anesthetize our minds to the point that we live in a state of constant denial, never admitting to ourselves that we have sinned. But God knows . . . and He punishes sin just as surely as He rewards righteousness.

Sins of all shapes and sizes have the power to do us great harm. And in a world where sin is big business, that's certainly a sobering thought. So do yourself and your loved ones a favor: conquer sin before it conquers you.

A LESSON TO THINK ABOUT

Every day of your life, you will be tempted to rebel against God's teachings. Your job, simply put, is to guard your heart against the darkness as you focus on the light.

WHAT GOD'S WORD SAYS ABOUT SIN

But now being made free from sin, and become servants to God, ye have your fruit unto holiness, and the end everlasting life. For the wages of sin is death; but the gift of God is eternal life through Jesus Christ our Lord.

Romans 6:22-23 KJV

It is written: There is no one righteous, not even one.

Romans 3:10 Holman CSB

The one who conceals his sins will not prosper, but whoever confesses and renounces them will find mercy.

Proverbs 28:13 Holman CSB

Disaster pursues sinners, but good rewards the righteous.

Proverbs 13:21 Holman CSB

WORDS OF WISDOM ABOUT
SIN

Sin promises freedom, but it only brings slavery.

Warren Wiersbe

We cannot out-sin God's ability to forgive us.

Beth Moore

As I have continued to grow in my Christian maturity, I have discovered that the Holy Spirit does not let me get by with anything.

Anne Graham Lotz

Every sin is a fall, and every fall is downward.

R. G. Lee

He loved us even while we were yet sinners at war with Him!

Bill Bright

Notes to Yourself: _____

_____

_____

_____

_____

_____

_____

_____

_____

_____

_____

_____

_____

As you consider the things you've written in the space above, ask yourself these questions:

Am I aware that the potential for sin is inevitably woven into the fabric of human existence?

Do I always think about the way that my behavior will impact my family, my friends, and my community?

Do I listen carefully to my conscience, and do I make sure that my actions are congruent with my beliefs?

WHEN YOU HAVE SINNED, REPENT

So David said to Nathan,
"I have sinned against the Lord."
And Nathan said to David,
"The Lord also has put away your sin; you shall not die."

2 Samuel 12:13 NKJV

The Message

When the prophet Nathan confronted David about his sins against Uriah—and against God—David confessed and repented. The Lord spared David.

Because he was a prophet, Nathan had a duty to confront sin, but it could not have been easy for Nathan to approach David. After all, David was king, a man who held the power to punish Nathan, or even to kill him. Despite these dangers, Nathan used a parable to show David the evil of his ways. Nathan's story touched David's heart, the king was remorseful, and he repented from his sins. And God forgave David.

God did not protect David from the consequences of his sins—to the contrary, David's transgressions brought untold suffering to his loved ones. But God refused to kill David because the king was genuinely sorry for his sins.

> *There will be more joy in heaven over one sinner who repents than over 99 righteous people who don't need repentance.*
> *Luke 15:7 Holman CSB*

Like King David, all of us have sinned. But the good news is this: When we ask for God's forgiveness and turn our hearts to Him, He forgives us absolutely and completely.

Genuine repentance requires more than simply offering God apologies for our misdeeds. Real repentance may start with feelings of sorrow and remorse, but it ends only when we turn away from the sin that has heretofore distanced us from our Creator. In truth, we offer our most meaningful apologies to God, not with our words, but with our actions. As long as we are still engaged in sin, we may be "repenting," but we have not fully "repented."

Is there an aspect of your life that is distancing you from your God? If so, ask for His forgiveness, and—just as importantly—stop sinning. Then, wrap yourself in the protection of God's Word. When you do, you will be secure.

A LESSON TO THINK ABOUT

If you're engaged in behavior that is displeasing to God, repent today—tomorrow may be too late.

WHAT GOD'S WORD SAYS ABOUT REPENTANCE

If we say, "We have no sin," we are deceiving ourselves, and the truth is not in us. If we confess our sins, He is faithful and righteous to forgive us our sins and to cleanse us from all unrighteousness.

1 John 1:8-9 Holman CSB

As obedient children, do not be conformed to the desires of your former ignorance but, as the One who called you is holy, you also are to be holy in all your conduct.

1 Peter 1:14-15 Holman CSB

All the prophets testify about Him that through His name everyone who believes in Him will receive forgiveness of sins.

Acts 10:43 Holman CSB

If My people who are called by My name will humble themselves, and pray and seek My face, and turn from their wicked ways, then I will hear from heaven, and will forgive their sin and heal their land.

2 Chronicles 7:14 NKJV

Words of Wisdom About
Repentance

True repentance is admitting that what God says is true, and that because it is true, we change our minds about our sins and about the Savior.

Warren Wiersbe

Sorrow for sin is as indispensable as faith.

C. H. Spurgeon

When true repentance comes, God will not hesitate for a moment to forgive, cast the sins in the sea of forgetfulness, and put the child on the road to restoration.

Beth Moore

Repentance begins with confession of our guilt and recognition that our sin is against God.

Charles Stanley

In repentance, we must be truly sorry for our sin, and we must express our intent to turn away from it.

Shirley Dobson

Notes to Yourself: _____

_____

_____

_____

_____

_____

_____

_____

_____

_____

_____

_____

_____

As you consider the things you've written in the space above, ask yourself these questions:

When I make mistakes, am I genuinely sorry?

When necessary, am I quick to seek forgiveness from others . . . and from God?

Do I understand that genuine repentance requires more than apologies—do I understand that real repentance requires me to change the behavior that I am apologizing for?

GOD WILL PROTECT YOU

And he said: "The Lord is my rock and my fortress and my deliverer; The God of my strength, in whom I will trust; My shield and the horn of my salvation, My stronghold and my refuge; My Savior, You save me from violence. I will call upon the Lord, who is worthy to be praised; So shall I be saved from my enemies."

2 Samuel 22:2-4 NKJV

The Message

After leading the Israelites in a great victory over the Philistines, David gave the credit to God. David understood that God was his fortress and his protector.

David realized that God was his shield, his protector, and his salvation. And if we're wise, we realize it, too. After all, God has promised to protect us, and He intends to keep His promise.

In a world filled with dangers and temptations, God is the ultimate armor. In a world filled with misleading messages, God's Word is the ultimate truth. In a world filled with more frustrations than we can count, God's Son offers the ultimate peace.

Will you accept God's peace and wear God's armor against the dangers of our world? Hopefully so—because when you do, you can live courageously, knowing that you possess the supreme protection: God's unfailing love for you.

> The Rock of Ages is the great sheltering encirclement.
> *Oswald Chambers*

The world offers no safety nets, but God does. He sent His only begotten Son to offer you the priceless gift of eternal life. And now you are challenged to return God's love by obeying His commandments and honoring His Son.

Sometimes, in the crush of everyday life, God may seem far away, but He is not. God is everywhere you have ever been and everywhere you will ever go. He is with you night and day; He knows your thoughts and your prayers. And, when you earnestly seek His protection, you will find it because He is here—always—waiting patiently for you to reach out to Him. And the next move, of course, is yours.

A LESSON TO THINK ABOUT

Earthly security is an illusion. Your only real security comes from the loving heart of God.

WHAT GOD'S WORD SAYS ABOUT GOD'S PROTECTION

The Lord bless you and protect you; the Lord make His face shine on you, and be gracious to you.

Numbers 6:24-25 Holman CSB

I know whom I have believed and am persuaded that He is able to guard what has been entrusted to me until that day.

2 Timothy 1:12 Holman CSB

For the LORD your God has arrived to live among you. He is a mighty savior. He will rejoice over you with great gladness. With his love, he will calm all your fears. He will exult over you by singing a happy song.

Zephaniah 3:17 Holman CSB

God—His way is perfect; the word of the Lord is pure. He is a shield to all who take refuge in Him.

Psalm 18:30 Holman CSB

The Lord is my rock, my fortress, and my deliverer.

Psalm 18:2 Holman CSB

WORDS OF WISDOM ABOUT
GOD'S PROTECTION

A mighty fortress is our God, a bulwark never failing
Our helper He, amid the flood of mortal ills prevailing
For still our ancient foe doth seek to work us woe
His craft and power are great, armed with cruel hate,
Our earth is not his equal.

Martin Luther

We are never out of reach of Satan's devices, so we must
never be without the whole armor of God.

Warren Wiersbe

God will never let you sink under your circumstances. He
always provides a safety net and His love always encircles.

Barbara Johnson

A God wise enough to create me and the world I live in is
wise enough to watch out for me.

Philip Yancey

Notes to Yourself: _____

_____

_____

_____

_____

_____

_____

_____

_____

_____

_____

_____

_____

As you consider the things you've written in the space above, ask yourself these questions:

Do I believe that God will protect me now and throughout eternity?

Do I trust God's plans even when I cannot understand them?

Am I willing to accept God's unfolding plan for the world—and for my world?

GOD REWARDS RIGHTEOUSNESS

The Lord rewarded me according to my righteousness;
According to the cleanness of my hands He has recompensed me.
For I have kept the ways of the Lord,
And have not wickedly departed from my God.

2 Samuel 22:21-22 NKJV

The Message

In a song of thanksgiving, David acknowledged that God had rewarded the righteous . . . and we can be certain that God still does.

David understood an important truth: God rewards righteousness. And it's a reality that we, as citizens of our temptation-filled world, must understand, too. When we seek righteousness in our own lives—and when we seek the companionship of those who do likewise—we reap the spiritual rewards that God intends for our lives. When we behave ourselves as godly men and women, we honor God. When we live righteously and according to God's commandments, He blesses us in ways that we cannot fully understand.

Each new day presents countless opportunities to put God in first place . . . or not. When we honor Him by living according to His commandments, we earn for ourselves the abundance and peace that He promises. But, when we concern ourselves more with pleasing others than with pleasing our Creator, we bring needless suffering upon ourselves and our families. Would you like a time-tested formula for successful living? Here is a formula that is proven and true: Seek God's approval in every aspect of your life. Does this sound too simple? Perhaps it is simple, but it is also the only way to reap the marvelous riches that God has in store for you.

> *Discipline yourself*
> *for the purpose*
> *of godliness.*
> 1 Timothy 4:7 NASB

So today, take every step of your journey with God as your traveling companion. Read His Word and follow His commandments. Support only those activities that further God's kingdom and your spiritual growth. Be an example of righteous living to your friends, to your neighbors, and to your children. Then, reap the blessings that God has promised to all those who live according to His will and His Word.

A LESSON TO THINK ABOUT

Because God is just, He rewards good behavior just as surely as He punishes sin. Obedience earns God's pleasure; disobedience doesn't.

WHAT GOD'S WORD SAYS ABOUT RIGHTEOUSNESS

For the eyes of the Lord are on the righteous, and His ears are open to their prayers; but the face of the Lord is against those who do evil.

1 Peter 3:12 NKJV

Walk in a manner worthy of the God who calls you into His own kingdom and glory.

1 Thessalonians 2:12 NASB

Run away from infantile indulgence. Run after mature righteousness—faith, love, peace—joining those who are in honest and serious prayer before God.

2 Timothy 2:22 MSG

And you shall do what is right and good in the sight of the Lord, that it may be well with you.

Deuteronomy 6:18 NKJV

WORDS OF WISDOM ABOUT RIGHTEOUSNESS

A man who lives right, and is right, has more power in his silence than another has by his words.

Phillips Brooks

He doesn't need an abundance of words. He doesn't need a dissertation about your life. He just wants your attention. He wants your heart.

Kathy Troccoli

As you walk by faith, you live a righteous life, for righteousness is always by faith.

Kay Arthur

If we don't hunger and thirst after righteousness, we'll become anemic and feel miserable in our Christian experience.

Franklin Graham

A life lived in God is not lived on the plane of feelings, but of the will.

Elisabeth Elliot

Notes to Yourself: _____

_____

_____

_____

_____

_____

_____

_____

_____

_____

_____

_____

_____

_____

As you consider the things you've written in the space above, ask yourself these questions:

Will I study God's Word each day, and will I strive to understand God's teachings?

Will I seek to live in accordance with Biblical teachings?

Will I, to the best of my abilities, surround myself with like-minded believers who seek to obey God's Word?

GOD WILL GUIDE YOUR STEPS

For You are my lamp, O Lord;
The Lord shall enlighten my darkness.

2 Samuel 22:29 NKJV

The Message

When David experienced the inevitable dark days of life,
he knew that God would be his light and his salvation.

When confronted with the inevitable dark days of life, David turned to God for guidance—and if we are wise, we will do the same. When we genuinely seek to know God's will—when we prayerfully seek His wisdom and His guidance—our Heavenly Father carefully leads us over the peaks and valleys of life. And as Christians, we can be comforted: Whether we find ourselves at the pinnacle of the mountain or the darkest depths of the valley, God is always there with us.

C. S. Lewis observed, "I don't doubt that the Holy Spirit guides your decisions from within when you make them with the intention of pleasing God. The error would be to think that He speaks only within, whereas in reality He speaks also through Scripture, the Church, Christian friends, and books." These words remind us that God has many ways to make Himself known. Our challenge is to make ourselves open to His instruction.

> If we want to hear God's voice, we must surrender our minds and hearts to Him.
>
> *Billy Graham*

Do you place a high value on God's guidance, and do you talk to Him regularly about matters great and small? Or do you talk with God on a haphazard basis? If you're wise, you'll form the habit of speaking to God early and often. But you won't stop there—you'll also study God's Word, you'll obey God's commandments, and you'll associate with people who do likewise.

So, if you're unsure of your next step, lean upon God's promises and lift your prayers to Him. Remember that God is always near—always trying to get His message through. Open yourself to Him every day, and trust Him to guide your path. When you do, you'll be protected today, tomorrow, and forever.

A LESSON TO THINK ABOUT

If you want God's guidance, ask for it. When you pray for guidance, God will give it.

WHAT GOD'S WORD SAYS ABOUT GOD'S GUIDANCE

Every morning he wakes me. He teaches me to listen like a student. The Lord God helps me learn . . . .

Isaiah 50:4-5 NCV

The Lord says, "I will make you wise and show you where to go. I will guide you and watch over you."

Psalm 32:8 NCV

The true children of God are those who let God's Spirit lead them.

Romans 8:14 NCV

Lord, You light my lamp; my God illuminates my darkness.

Psalm 18:28 Holman CSB

In all your ways acknowledge Him, and He shall direct your paths.

Proverbs 3:6 NKJV

WORDS OF WISDOM ABOUT
GOD'S GUIDANCE

It is a joy that God never abandons His children. He guides faithfully all who listen to His directions.

Corrie ten Boom

Enjoy the adventure of receiving God guidance. Taste it, revel in it, appreciate the fact that the journey is often a lot more exciting than arriving at the destination.

Bill Hybels

God's leading will never be contrary to His word.

Vonette Bright

Are you serious about wanting God's guidance to become a personal reality in your life? The first step is to tell God that you know you can't manage your own life; that you need his help.

Catherine Marshall

Notes to Yourself: _____

_____

_____

_____

_____

_____

_____

_____

_____

_____

_____

_____

_____

As you consider the things you've written in the space above, ask yourself these questions:

Do I seek God's guidance in every aspect of my life?

Do I allow God to guide me by His word and by His Spirit?

Do I talk to God often, and, just as importantly, do I listen to Him often?

LESSON 10

GOD IS
YOUR
SHEPHERD

*The LORD is my shepherd; I shall not want. He maketh me
to lie down in green pastures: he leadeth me beside the still
waters. He restoreth my soul: he leadeth me in the paths of
righteousness for his name's sake. Yea, though I walk through
the valley of the shadow of death, I will fear no evil: for thou art
with me; thy rod and thy staff they comfort me. Thou preparest
a table before me in the presence of mine enemies: thou anointest
my head with oil; my cup runneth over. Surely goodness
and mercy shall follow me all the days of my life:
and I will dwell in the house of the LORD for ever.*

Psalm 23 KJV

Open your Bible to its center, and you'll find the Book of Psalm. In it are some of the most beautiful words ever translated into the English language, with none more beautiful than the 23rd Psalm. David describes God as being like a shepherd who cares for His flock. No wonder these verses have provided comfort and hope for generations of believers.

> Like a shadow declining
> swiftly . . . away . . .
> like the dew of the
> morning gone with the
> heat of the day;
> like the wind in the
> treetops, like a wave
> of the sea, so are
> our lives on earth
> when seen in light
> of eternity.
>
> *Ruth Bell Graham*

You are precious in the eyes of God. You are His priceless creation, made in His image, and protected by Him. God watches over every step you make and every breath you take, so you need never be afraid. But sometimes, fear has a way of slipping into the minds and hearts of even the most devout believers. You are no exception.

On occasion, you will confront circumstances that trouble you to the very core of your soul. When you are afraid, trust in God. When you are worried, turn your concerns over to Him. When you are anxious, be still and listen for the quiet assurance of God's promises. And then, place your life in His hands. He is your shepherd today and throughout eternity. Trust the Shepherd.

A LESSON TO THINK ABOUT

Your life is a priceless opportunity, a gift of incalculable worth. You should thank God for the gift of life . . . and you should use that gift wisely.

WHAT GOD'S WORD SAYS ABOUT LIFE

Watch your life and doctrine closely. Persevere in them, because if you do, you will save both yourself and your hearers.

1 Timothy 4:16 NIV

His divine power has given us everything we need for life and godliness through our knowledge of him who called us by his own glory and goodness.

2 Peter 1:3 NIV

Seek the Lord, and ye shall live . . . .

Amos 5:6 KJV

I urge you to live a life worthy of the calling you have received.

Ephesians 4:1 NIV

And Jesus said unto them, I am the bread of life: he that cometh to me shall never hunger; and he that believeth on me shall never thirst.

John 6:35 KJV

WORDS OF WISDOM ABOUT
LIFE

The value of a life can only be estimated by its relationship to God.

Oswald Chambers

Jesus wants Life for us, Life with a capital L.

John Eldredge

The world has never been stable. Jesus Himself was born into the cruelest and most unstable of worlds. No, we have babies and keep trusting and living because the Resurrection is true! The Resurrection was not just a one-time event in history; it is a principle built into the very fabric of our beings, a fact reverberating from every cell of creation: Life wins! Life wins!

Gloria Gaither

A life lived without reflection can be very superficial and empty.

Elisabeth Elliot

Notes to Yourself: _____

_____

_____

_____

_____

_____

_____

_____

_____

_____

_____

_____

_____

As you consider the things you've written in the space above, ask yourself these questions:

Do I consider my life to be a priceless gift from God?

Do I spend time each day thanking God for His blessings?

Do I slow down to marvel at the beauty of God's glorious creation?

WHEN YOU FEAR GOD, YOU CAN LIVE FEARLESSLY

The Lord is my light and my salvation—
whom should I fear?
The Lord is the stronghold of my life—
of whom should I be afraid?

Psalm 27:1 Holman CSB

The Message

David understood that our greatest fear should be the fear of displeasing God. When we have a healthy fear of our Creator, all other fears are kept in check.

David understood that when we trust God completely and without reservation, our fears can no longer control us. But if we fail to place our trust in God, for whatever reason, our fears—whether rational or imagined—have the power to dominate our thoughts and our lives.

We live in a fear-based world, a world where bad news travels at light speed and good news doesn't. These are troubled times, times when we have legitimate fears for the future of our nation, our world, and our families. But as Christians, we have every reason to live courageously. After all, the ultimate battle has already been fought and won on that faraway cross at Calvary.

> When we meditate on God and remember the promises He has given us in His Word, our faith grows, and our fears dissolve.
>
> *Charles Stanley*

When we focus upon our fears and our doubts, we may find many reasons to lie awake at night and fret about the uncertainties of the coming day. A better strategy, of course, is to focus not upon our fears, but instead upon our God.

Perhaps you, like countless other believers, have found your courage tested by the anxieties and panics that have become an inevitable part of 21st-century life. If so, God wants to have a little chat with you. The next time you find your courage tested to the limit, God wants to remind you that He is not just near; He is here.

Your Heavenly Father is your Protector and your Deliverer. Call upon Him in your hour of need, and be comforted. Whatever your challenge, whatever your trouble, God can handle it. And will.

A LESSON TO THINK ABOUT

If you're feeling fearful or anxious, you must trust God to solve the problems that are simply too big for you to solve.

WHAT GOD'S WORD SAYS ABOUT FEAR

Don't be afraid, because I am your God. I will make you strong and will help you; I will support you with my right hand that saves you.

Isaiah 41:10 NCV

Don't be afraid, because the Lord your God will be with you everywhere you go.

Joshua 1:9 NCV

Be strong and courageous, and do the work. Do not be afraid or discouraged, for the Lord God, my God, is with you.

1 Chronicles 28:20 NIV

That is why we can say with confidence, "The Lord is my helper, so I will not be afraid. What can mere mortals do to me?"

Hebrews 13:6 NLT

I sought the LORD, and he answered me; he delivered me from all my fears.

Psalm 34:4 NIV

Words of Wisdom About
Fear

Fear is a self-imposed prison that will keep you from becoming what God intends for you to be.

Rick Warren

The Bible is a Christian's guidebook, and I believe the knowledge it sheds on pain and suffering is the great antidote to fear for suffering people. Knowledge can dissolve fear as light destroys darkness.

Philip Yancey

God shields us from most of the things we fear, but when He chooses not to shield us, He unfailingly allots grace in the measure needed.

Elisabeth Elliot

Only believe, don't fear. Our Master, Jesus, always watches over us, and no matter what the persecution, Jesus will surely overcome it.

Lottie Moon

Notes to Yourself: _____

_____

_____

_____

_____

_____

_____

_____

_____

_____

_____

_____

_____

As you consider the things you've written in the space above, ask yourself these questions:

When I am fearful, do I take my concerns to God in prayer?

Do I consider God to be a partner in every aspect of my life?

Will I trust God to handle the problems that are simply too big for me to solve?

Lesson 12

Wait for the Lord

Wait for the Lord; be courageous and let your heart be strong.
Wait for the Lord.

Psalm 27:14 Holman CSB

The Message

David instructs us to trust God's timetable—we should wait patiently for the Lord to reveal His plans.

King David understood the need for patience, and so must we. But for most of us, patience is a difficult thing to master. Why? Because we have lots of things we want, and we know precisely when we want them: NOW (if not sooner). Yet our Father in heaven often has other ideas; the Bible teaches that we must learn to wait patiently for the things that God has in store for us, even when waiting is difficult.

We live in an imperfect world inhabited by imperfect people. Sometimes, we inherit troubles from others, and sometimes we create troubles for ourselves. On other occasions, we see other people "moving ahead" in the world, and we want to move ahead with them. So we become impatient with ourselves, with our circumstances, and even with our Creator.

> Waiting means going about our assigned tasks, confident that God will provide the meaning and the conclusions.
>
> *Eugene Peterson*

In Psalm 37:7 David teaches us to "rest in the Lord, and wait patiently for Him" (NKJV). But, for most of us, waiting patiently for Him is hard. We are fallible human beings who seek solutions to our problems today, not tomorrow. Still, God instructs us to wait patiently for His plans to unfold, and that's exactly what we should do.

Sometimes, patience is the price we pay for being responsible adults, and that's as it should be. After all, think how patient our Heavenly Father has been with us. So the next time you find yourself drumming your fingers as you wait for a quick resolution to the challenges of everyday living, take a deep breath and ask God for patience. Be still before your Heavenly Father and trust His timetable: it's the peaceful way to live.

A LESSON TO THINK ABOUT

Patience pays. Impatience costs. Behave accordingly.

WHAT GOD'S WORD SAYS ABOUT PATIENCE

We urge you, brethren, admonish the unruly, encourage the fainthearted, help the weak, be patient with everyone.

1 Thessalonians 5:14 NASB

Be completely humble and gentle; be patient, bearing with one another in love.

Ephesians 4:2 NIV

Wherefore seeing we also are compassed about with so great a cloud of witnesses, let us lay aside every weight, and the sin which doth so easily beset us, and let us run with patience the race that is set before us . . . .

Hebrews 12:1 KJV

Yet the LORD longs to be gracious to you; he rises to show you compassion. For the LORD is a God of justice. Blessed are all who wait for him!

Isaiah 30:18 NIV

A person's insight gives him patience, and his virtue is to overlook an offense.

Proverbs 19:11 Holman CSB

WORDS OF WISDOM ABOUT PATIENCE

Waiting is an essential part of spiritual discipline. It can be the ultimate test of faith.

Anne Graham Lotz

No matter what we are going through, no matter how long the waiting for answers, of one thing we may be sure. God is faithful. He keeps His promises. What He starts, He finishes . . . including His perfect work in us.

Gloria Gaither

Let God use times of waiting to mold and shape your character. Let God use those times to purify your life and make you into a clean vessel for His service.

Henry Blackaby and Claude King

To receive the blessing we need, we must believe and keep on believing, and we must also wait and keep on waiting. We need to wait in prayer, wait with our Bibles open as we confess his promises, wait in joyful praise and worship of the God who will never forget our case, and wait as we continue serving others in his name.

Jim Cymbala

Notes to Yourself: _____

_____

_____

_____

_____

_____

_____

_____

_____

_____

_____

_____

As you consider the things you've written in the space above, ask yourself these questions:

Do I take seriously the Bible's instructions to be patient?

Do I believe that patience is not idle waiting but that it is an activity that means watching and waiting for God to lead me in the direction of His choosing?

Even when I don't understand the circumstances that confront me, do I strive to wait patiently while serving the Lord?

YOU ARE "WONDERFULLY MADE" BY THE CREATOR

I will praise You, for I am fearfully and wonderfully made;
Marvelous are Your works, And that my soul knows very well.

Psalm 139:14 NKJV

The Message

David knew that he, like every human being, was "wonderfully made" by God. You should know it, too. God made you—and God loves you. That means you are a marvelous part of God's creation, and it means you have great worth.

Do you like the person you see when you look into the mirror? You should! After all, the person in the mirror is a very special person who is made—and loved—by God. And God knew precisely what He was doing when He gave you a unique set of talents and opportunities. Now, it's up to you to discover those talents and to use them, but sometimes the world will encourage you to do otherwise. At times, society will attempt to force you into a particular, preformed mold. Yet God may have other plans in store for you.

> Give yourself a gift today: be present with yourself. God is. Enjoy your own personality. God does.
>
> *Barbara Johnson*

The world will attempt to define you—how you should look, how you should act, and how you should think. And, because you're an imperfect human being, you may become so wrapped up in meeting the world's expectations that you fail to focus on God's expectations. To do so is a mistake of major proportions—don't make it. Instead of trying to please the world, try to please God by becoming the very best "you" that you can possibly be.

Thousands of books have been written about ways to improve self-esteem. Yet, maintaining a healthy self-image is, to a surprising extent, a matter of doing three things:

1. Obeying God; 2. Thinking healthy thoughts; 3. Finding a purpose for your life that pleases your Creator and yourself.

Finally, here's a word of caution: don't spend too much time focusing on self-esteem: Instead, you should focus on using your talents and pleasing your God. You should learn to direct your thoughts in positive ways. You should strive to find something to do and someone to love. When you accomplish these things, your self-esteem will, on most days, take care of itself.

A LESSON TO THINK ABOUT

Old-fashioned respect never goes out of style—respect for other people and respect for the person in the mirror. You are incredibly special to God. Are you incredibly special to yourself?

WHAT GOD'S WORD SAYS ABOUT SELF-WORTH

For you made us only a little lower than God, and you crowned us with glory and honor.

Psalm 8:5 NLT

God began doing a good work in you, and I am sure he will continue it until it is finished when Jesus Christ comes again.

Philippians 1:6 NCV

For You formed my inward parts; You covered me in my mother's womb. I will praise You, for I am fearfully and wonderfully made; Marvelous are Your works.

Psalm 139:13-14 NKJV

You're blessed when you're content with just who you are—no more, no less. That's the moment you find yourselves proud owners of everything that can't be bought.

Matthew 5:5 MSG

To acquire wisdom is to love oneself; people who cherish understanding will prosper.

Proverbs 19:8 NLT

WORDS OF WISDOM ABOUT
SELF-WORTH

You are valuable just because you exist. Not because of what you do or what you have done, but simply because you are.

Max Lucado

If you ever put a price tag on yourself, it would have to read "Jesus" because that is what God paid to save you.

Josh McDowell

Being loved by Him whose opinion matters most gives us the security to risk loving, too—even loving ourselves.

Gloria Gaither

Find satisfaction in him who made you, and only then find satisfaction in yourself as part of his creation.

St. Augustine

Notes to Yourself: _____

_____

_____

_____

_____

_____

_____

_____

_____

_____

_____

_____

As you consider the things you've written in the space above, ask yourself these questions:

Do I pay careful attention to the messages that I'm sending myself about myself?

Am I sometimes my own worst critic, and is the criticism really deserved?

Do I remind myself that God loves me . . . and that I should, too?

GOD BLESSES THOSE WHO TRUST HIM

Oh, taste and see that the Lord is good;
Blessed is the man who trusts in Him!

Psalm 34:8 NKJV

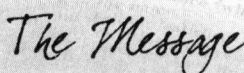

The Message

David instructs us to trust God—when we do so, we are blessed.

David counted his blessings, and so should you. Your blessings include life, freedom, family, friends, talents, and possessions, for starters. But, your greatest blessing—a gift that is yours for the asking—is God's gift of salvation through Christ Jesus.

Are you a thankful believer who takes time each day to take a partial inventory of the gifts God has given you? Hopefully you are that kind of Christian. After all, God's Word makes it clear: a wise heart is a thankful heart.

We honor God, in part, by the genuine gratitude we feel in our hearts for the blessings He has bestowed upon us. Yet even the most saintly among us must endure periods of fear, doubt, and regret. Why? Because we are imperfect human beings who are incapable of perfect gratitude. Still, even on life's darker days, we must seek to cleanse our hearts of negative emotions and fill them, instead, with praise, with love, with hope, and with thanksgiving. To do otherwise is to be unfair to ourselves, to our loved ones, and to our God.

> It is when we give ourselves to be a blessing that we can especially count on the blessing of God.
>
> *Andrew Murray*

Sometimes, life-here-on-earth can be complicated, demanding, and frustrating. When the demands of life leave us rushing from place to place with scarcely a moment to spare, we may fail to pause and thank our Creator for His gifts. But, whenever we neglect to give proper thanks to the Father, we suffer because of our misplaced priorities.

Today, begin making a list of your blessings. You most certainly will not be able to make a complete list, but take a few moments and jot down as many blessings as you can. Then, give thanks to the Giver of all good things: God. His love for you is eternal, as are His gifts. And it's never too soon—or too late—to offer Him thanks.

A LESSON TO THINK ABOUT

God wants to bless you abundantly and eternally. When you trust God completely and obey Him faithfully, you will be blessed.

WHAT GOD'S WORD SAYS ABOUT
GOD'S BLESSING

I will give you a new heart and put a new spirit within you.

Ezekiel 36:26 Holman CSB

The Lord bless you and protect you; the Lord make His face shine on you, and be gracious to you.

Numbers 6:24-25 Holman CSB

Blessings are on the head of the righteous.

Proverbs 10:6 Holman CSB

Come to terms with God and be at peace; in this way good will come to you.

Job 22:21 Holman CSB

Blessed is a man who endures trials, because when he passes the test he will receive the crown of life that He has promised to those who love Him.

James 1:12 Holman CSB

WORDS OF WISDOM ABOUT
GOD'S BLESSING

Grace is an outrageous blessing bestowed freely on a totally undeserving recipient.

Bill Hybels

God's love for His children is unconditional, no strings attached. But, God's blessings on our lives do come with a condition—obedience. If we are to receive the fullness of God's blessings, we must obey Him and keep His commandments.

Jim Gallery

With the goodness of God to desire our highest welfare and the wisdom of God to plan it, what do we lack? Surely we are the most favored of all creatures.

A. W. Tozer

Grace comes from the heart of a gracious God who wants to stun you and overwhelm you with a gift you don't deserve—salvation, adoption, a spiritual ability to use in kingdom service, answered prayer, the church, His presence, His wisdom, His guidance, His love.

Bill Hybels

Notes to Yourself: _____

_____

_____

_____

_____

_____

_____

_____

_____

_____

_____

_____

As you consider the things you've written in the space above, ask yourself these questions:

Do I take time every day to thank God for His blessings?

Do I expect God to continue to bless me now and forever?

Am I willing to put problems in perspective by overlooking the minor inconveniences of life, or am I often tempted to focus on negatives instead of positives?

DON'T
GIVE IN

*I waited patiently for the Lord;
And He inclined to me, And heard my cry.*

Psalm 40:1 NKJV

The Message

David teaches us to wait patiently for God . . . and to keep working while we do.

A s you continue to seek God's purpose for your life, you will undoubtedly experience your fair share of disappointments, detours, false starts, and failures. When you do, don't become discouraged: God's not finished with you yet.

The old saying is as true today as it was when it was first spoken: "Life is a marathon, not a sprint." That's why wise travelers (like you) select a traveling companion who never tires and never falters. That partner, of course, is your Heavenly Father.

> So we must not get
> tired of doing good,
> for we will reap
> at the proper time
> if we don't give up.
> Galatians 6:9 Holman CSB

The next time you find your courage tested to the limit, remember that God is as near as your next breath, and remember that He offers strength and comfort to His children. He is your shield and your strength; He is your protector and your deliverer. Call upon Him in your hour of need and then be comforted. Whatever your challenge, whatever your trouble, God can help you persevere. And that's precisely what He'll do if you ask Him.

King David understood the importance of perseverance. And he understood the wisdom of waiting for God to reveal

His plans. Are you willing to keep working—and praying—
even during life's darker days? If so, you'll be rewarded for
your patience and your perseverance. And who knows? Your
rewards may start coming even sooner than you think.

A LESSON TO THINK ABOUT

Life is an exercise in perseverance. If you persevere, you
win.

WHAT GOD'S WORD SAYS ABOUT PERSEVERANCE

For you need endurance, so that after you have done God's will, you may receive what was promised.

Hebrews 10:36 Holman CSB

Do you not know that the runners in a stadium all race, but only one receives the prize? Run in such a way that you may win. Now everyone who competes exercises self-control in everything. However, they do it to receive a perishable crown, but we an imperishable one.

1 Corinthians 9:24-25 Holman CSB

Pursue righteousness, godliness, faith, love, endurance, and gentleness. Fight the good fight for the faith; take hold of eternal life, to which you were called and have made a good confession before many witnesses.

1 Timothy 6:11-12 Holman CSB

But as for you, be strong; don't be discouraged, for your work has a reward.

2 Chronicles 15:7 Holman CSB

WORDS OF WISDOM ABOUT PERSEVERANCE

Keep adding, keep walking, keep advancing; do not stop, do not turn back, do not turn from the straight road.

St. Augustine

In the Bible, patience is not a passive acceptance of circumstances. It is a courageous perseverance in the face of suffering and difficulty.

Warren Wiersbe

Battles are won in the trenches, in the grit and grime of courageous determination; they are won day by day in the arena of life.

Charles Swindoll

Failure is one of life's most powerful teachers. How we handle our failures determines whether we're going to simply "get by" in life or "press on."

Beth Moore

Perseverance is more than endurance. It is endurance combined with absolute assurance and certainty that what we are looking for is going to happen.

Oswald Chambers

Notes to Yourself: _____

_____

_____

_____

_____

_____

_____

_____

_____

_____

_____

_____

As you consider the things you've written in the space above, ask yourself these questions:

Do I have a healthy respect for the power of perseverance?

When I am discouraged, do I ask God to give me strength?

Do I associate with people who encourage me to be courageous, optimistic, energetic, and persistent?

GOD WILL RENEW YOUR STRENGTH

He also brought me up out of a horrible pit,
out of the miry clay, and set my feet upon a rock,
and established my steps. He has put a new song
in my mouth—praise to our God; many will see it and fear,
and will trust in the Lord.

Psalm 40:2-3 NKJV

The Message

David proclaims that God has the power to save you from the darkness, to put a new song on your lips, and to restore your spirits.

In the 40th Psalm, David rejoiced because God has delivered David from sorrow while putting a new song on David's lips. Perhaps you, like David, are enduring the inevitable dark days of life. If so, you must remember that God can renew your spirit, just like He renewed David's.

Even if you're an inspired believer, even if you're normally upbeat about your future and your life, you may, on occasion, find yourself running on empty. The demands of daily life can drain you of your strength and rob you of the joy that is rightfully yours in Christ. When you are tired, discouraged, or despondent, there is a source from which you can draw the power needed to recharge your spiritual batteries. That source is God.

> Repentance removes old sins and wrong attitudes, and it opens the way for the Holy Spirit to restore our spiritual health.
>
> *Shirley Dobson*

God intends that you lead a life of abundance and peace. But sometimes, abundance and peace seem very far away. It is then that you must turn to God for renewal, and when you do, He will restore you.

Are you tired or troubled? Turn your heart toward God in prayer. Are you weak or worried? Take the time—or, more accurately, make the time—to delve deeply into God's Holy Word. Are you spiritually depleted? Call upon fellow believers to support you, and call upon Christ to renew your spirit and your life. When you do, you'll discover that the Creator of the universe stands always ready and always able to create a new sense of wonderment and joy in you.

A LESSON TO THINK ABOUT

God can make all things new, including you. When you are weak or worried, God can renew your spirit. Your task is to let Him.

WHAT GOD'S WORD SAYS ABOUT RENEWAL

The One who was sitting on the throne said, "Look! I am making everything new!" Then he said, "Write this, because these words are true and can be trusted."

Revelation 21:5 NCV

When doubts filled my mind, your comfort gave me renewed hope and cheer.

Psalm 94:19 NLT

Create in me a pure heart, O God, and renew a steadfast spirit within me. Do not cast me from your presence or take your Holy Spirit from me. Restore to me the joy of your salvation and grant me a willing spirit, to sustain me.

Psalm 51:10-12 NIV

He makes me to lie down in green pastures; He leads me beside the still waters. He restores my soul; He leads me in the paths of righteousness for His name's sake.

Psalm 23:2-3 NKJV

WORDS OF WISDOM ABOUT RENEWAL

In those desperate times when we feel like we don't have an ounce of strength, He will gently pick up our heads so that our eyes can behold something—something that will keep His hope alive in us.

Kathy Troccoli

He is the God of wholeness and restoration.

Stormie Omartian

Each of us has something broken in our lives: a broken promise, a broken dream, a broken marriage, a broken heart . . . and we must decide how we're going to deal with our brokenness. We can wallow in self-pity or regret, accomplishing nothing and having no fun or joy in our circumstances; or we can determine with our will to take a few risks, get out of our comfort zone, and see what God will do to bring unexpected delight in our time of need.

Luci Swindoll

Walking with God leads to receiving his intimate counsel, and counseling leads to deep restoration.

John Eldredge

Notes to Yourself: _____

_____

_____

_____

_____

_____

_____

_____

_____

_____

_____

_____

_____

As you consider the things you've written in the space above, ask yourself these questions:

Do I believe that God can make all things new—including me?

Do I take time each day to be still and let God give me perspective and direction?

Do I understand the importance of getting a good night's sleep?

YOU CAN OVERCOME ADVERSITY

*May the Lord answer you when you are in distress;
may the name of the God of Jacob protect you.*

Psalm 20:1 NIV

The Message

David understood that God is the ultimate armor, that
God protects those who love Him.

As life here on earth unfolds, all of us encounter occasional disappointments and setbacks: Those occasional visits from Old Man Trouble are simply a fact of life, and none of us are exempt. When tough times arrive, we may be forced to rearrange our plans and our priorities. But even on our darkest days, we must remember that God's love remains constant.

The fact that we encounter adversity is not nearly so important as the way we choose to deal with it. When tough times arrive, we have a clear choice: we can begin the difficult work of tackling our troubles . . . or not. When we summon the courage to look Old Man Trouble squarely in the eye, he usually blinks. But, if we refuse to address our problems, even the smallest annoyances have a way of growing into king-sized catastrophes.

Psalm 145, David promises, "The Lord is near to all who call on him, to all who call on him in truth. He fulfills the desires of those who fear him; he hears their cry and saves them" (vv. 18-20 NIV). And the words of Jesus offer us comfort: "These things I have spoken to you, that in Me

> If all struggles and sufferings were eliminated, the spirit would no more reach maturity than would the child.
>
> *Elisabeth Elliot*

you may have peace. In the world you will have tribulation; but be of good cheer, I have overcome the world" (John 16:33 NKJV).

As believers, we know that God loves us and that He will protect us. In times of hardship, He will comfort us; in times of sorrow, He will dry our tears. When we are troubled or weak or sorrowful, God is always with us. We must build our lives on the rock that cannot be shaken: we must trust in God. And then, we must get on with the hard work of tackling our problems . . . because if we don't, who will? Or should?

A LESSON TO THINK ABOUT

If you're going through difficult times, consider it an opportunity for spiritual growth. So ask yourself this question: "What is God trying to teach me today?"

What God's Word Says About Adversity

The Lord lifts the burdens of those bent beneath their loads. The Lord loves the righteous.

Psalm 146:8 NLT

No discipline seems pleasant at the time, but painful. Later on, however, it produces a harvest of righteousness and peace for those who have been trained by it.

Hebrews 12:11 NIV

For though a righteous man falls seven times, he rises again . . . .

Proverbs 24:16 NIV

Come to me, all you who are weary and burdened, and I will give you rest. Take my yoke upon you and learn from me, for I am gentle and humble in heart, and you will find rest for your souls. For my yoke is easy and my burden is light.

Matthew 11:28-30 NIV

WORDS OF WISDOM ABOUT ADVERSITY

Adversity is not simply a tool. It is God's most effective tool for the advancement of our spiritual lives. The circumstances and events that we see as setbacks are oftentimes the very things that launch us into periods of intense spiritual growth. Once we begin to understand this, and accept it as a spiritual fact of life, adversity becomes easier to bear.

Charles Stanley

Faith is a strong power, mastering any difficulty in the strength of the Lord who made heaven and earth.

Corrie ten Boom

The only way to learn a strong faith is to endure great trials. I have learned my faith by standing firm amid the most severe of tests.

George Mueller

Often the trials we mourn are really gateways into the good things we long for.

Hannah Whitall Smith

Notes to Yourself: _____

_____

_____

_____

_____

_____

_____

_____

_____

_____

_____

_____

As you consider the things you've written in the space above, ask yourself these questions:

When tough times arrive, am I willing to place my future in God's hands?

Am I willing to work hard to resolve my own problems, or do I expect other people to solve them for me?

When I face adversity, am I willing to talk things over with family, with trusted friends, and with God . . . or do I keep everything bottled up inside?

BE STILL
BEFORE GOD

I wait quietly before God, for my salvation comes from him.

Psalm 62:1 NLT

The Message

David understood the wisdom of waiting quietly before
God so that the Creator might reveal Himself.

David the king was once David the shepherd, so he understood the importance of spending time alone with God. In solitude, with sheep braying at his side and clouds passing silently overhead, young David must have come to treasure the quiet moments he shared with his Father in heaven. So it's no surprise that when David became a man, he still insisted upon spending quiet time with God—and so should we. But sometimes, here in the noisy 21st-century, we may find it difficult to find a quiet place to claim even a few minutes of silence.

> Be still:
> pause and discover
> that God is God.
>
> *Charles Swindoll*

The world seems to grow louder day by day, and our senses seem to be invaded at every turn. But, if we allow the distractions of a clamorous society to separate us from God's peace, we do ourselves a profound disservice. Our task, as dutiful believers, is to carve out moments of silence in a world filled with noise.

If we are to maintain righteous minds and compassionate hearts, we must take time each day for prayer and for meditation. We must make ourselves still in the presence of our Creator. We must quiet our minds and our hearts so that we might sense God's will and His love.

Has the busy pace of life robbed you of the peace that God has promised? If so, it's time to reorder your priorities and your life. Nothing is more important than the time you spend with your Heavenly Father. So be still and claim the inner peace that is found in the silent moments you spend with God. His peace is offered freely; it has been paid for in full; it is yours for the asking. So ask. And then share.

A LESSON TO THINK ABOUT

You live in a noisy world filled with distractions, a world where silence is in short supply. But God wants you to carve out quiet moments with Him. Silence is, indeed, golden.

WHAT GOD'S WORD SAYS ABOUT STILLNESS

Be still before the Lord and wait patiently for Him.

Psalm 37:7 NIV

In quietness and trust is your strength.

Isaiah 30:15 NASB

Be still, and know that I am God.

Psalm 46:10 NKJV

I wait quietly before God, for my hope is in him.

Psalm 62:5 NLT

What's this? Fools out shopping for wisdom! They wouldn't recognize it if they saw it! One Who Knows Much Says Little.

Proverbs 17:16 MSG

WORDS OF WISDOM ABOUT STILLNESS AND QUIET TIME

There are times when to speak is to violate the moment—when silence represents the highest respect. The word for such times is reverence.

Max Lucado

Let your loneliness be transformed into a holy aloneness. Sit still before the Lord. Remember Naomi's word to Ruth: "Sit still, my daughter, until you see how the matter will fall."

Elisabeth Elliot

Instead of waiting for the feeling, wait upon God. You can do this by growing still and quiet, then expressing in prayer what your mind knows is true about Him, even if your heart doesn't feel it at this moment.

Shirley Dobson

The remedy for distractions is the same now as it was in earlier and simpler times: prayer, meditation, and the cultivation of the inner life.

A. W. Tozer

Notes to Yourself: _____

_____

_____

_____

_____

_____

_____

_____

_____

_____

_____

_____

_____

As you consider the things you've written in the space above, ask yourself these questions:

Do I try to spend quiet moments with God every day of the week, or just on Sundays?

During the quiet moments of the day, can I sense that God is leading me in the direction He wants me to go?

When I have an important decision to make, do I quiet myself so that I can listen carefully to my conscience and, more importantly, to God?

YOU CAN SERVE GOD BY SERVING OTHERS

Lord, I give myself to you; my God, I trust you.

Psalm 25:1-2 NCV

The Message

David offered to give his heart and his service to God.

How can we serve God? By sharing His message, His mercy, and His love with those who cross our paths. Everywhere we look, it seems, the needs are great, and at every turn, or so it seems, so are the temptations. Still, our challenge is clear: we must love God, obey His commandments, trust His Son, and serve His children. When we place the Lord in His rightful place—at the center of our lives—then we claim spiritual treasures that will endure forever.

> *Serve the Lord with gladness.*
> Psalm 100:2 Holman CSB

If you genuinely seek to discover God's unfolding priorities for your life, you must ask yourself this question: "How does God want me to serve others?"

Whatever your path, whatever your calling, you may be certain of this: service to others is an integral part of God's plan for your life. Christ was the ultimate servant, the Savior who gave His life for mankind. As His followers, we, too, must become humble servants.

Are you willing to become a humble servant for Christ? Are you willing to roll up your sleeves and do your part to make the world a better place, or are you determined to keep all your blessings to yourself? The answer to these questions will determine the quantity and the quality of the service you render to God and to His children.

Today, you may feel the temptation to build yourself up in the eyes of your neighbors. Resist that temptation. Instead, serve your neighbors quietly and without fanfare. Find a need and fill it . . . humbly. Lend a helping hand and share a word of kindness . . . anonymously, for this is God's way.

As a humble servant, you will glorify yourself not before men, but before God, and that's what God intends. After all, earthly glory is fleeting: here today and all too soon gone. But, heavenly glory endures throughout eternity. So, the choice is yours: Either you can lift yourself up here on earth and be humbled in heaven, or vice versa. Please choose wisely.

A Lesson to Think About

Whether you realize it or not, God has called you to a life of service. Your job is to find a place to serve and to get busy.

What God's Word Says About Serving God

Be strong and of good courage, and do it; do not fear nor be dismayed, for the Lord God—my God—will be with you. He will not leave you nor forsake you, until you have finished all the work for the service of the house of the Lord.

1 Chronicles 28:20 NKJV

Let a man so consider us, as servants of Christ and stewards of the mysteries of God. Moreover it is required in stewards that one be found faithful.

1 Corinthians 4:1-2 NKJV

Worship the Lord your God and . . . serve Him only.

Matthew 4:10 Holman CSB

Well done, good and faithful servant; you were faithful over a few things, I will make you ruler over many things. Enter into the joy of your lord.

Matthew 25:21 NKJV

WORDS OF WISDOM ABOUT
SERVING GOD

God wants us to serve Him with a willing spirit, one that would choose no other way.

Beth Moore

No life can surpass that of a man who quietly continues to serve God in the place where providence has placed him.

C. H. Spurgeon

Have thy tools ready; God will find thee work.

Charles Kingsley

In the very place where God has put us, whatever its limitations, whatever kind of work it may be, we may indeed serve the Lord Christ.

Elisabeth Elliot

A Christian is a perfectly free lord of all, subject to none. A Christian is a perfectly dutiful servant of all, subject to all.

Martin Luther

Notes to Yourself: _____

_____

_____

_____

_____

_____

_____

_____

_____

_____

_____

_____

_____

_____

As you consider the things you've written in the space above, ask yourself these questions:

Am I willing to serve God by being a faithful steward of the talents He has entrusted to my care?

Do I believe that a willingness to serve others is a sign of greatness in God's eyes?

Do I believe that I am surrounded by opportunities to serve and that I should take advantage of those opportunities?

GOD CREATED THE UNIVERSE . . . AND YOU

The fool hath said in his heart, There is no God.

Psalm 14:1 KJV

The Message

David understood that wise people believe in God . . . and that foolish people deny the existence of God.

David knew that God exists . . . from personal, intimate, firsthand experience. So, when he came to address the existence of a Creator, David made his case in a straightforward manner: he said that only foolish people would attempt to deny the existence of God. What was true in David's time is equally true in our own. The evidence for God's existence is everywhere.

As we pause to examine God's wondrous handiwork, it quickly becomes apparent that God is, indeed, a miracle worker. Throughout history He has intervened in the course of human events in ways which can't be explained by science or human rationale. But God's miracles are not limited to special occasions, nor are they witnessed by a select few. God is crafting His wonders all around us: the miracle of the birth of a new baby; the miracle of a world renewing itself with every sunrise; the miracle of lives transformed by God's love and by His grace. Each day God's miraculous handiwork is evident for all to see and to experience.

> No philosophical theory which I have yet come across is a radical improvement on the words of Genesis, that "in the beginning God made Heaven and Earth."
>
> *C. S. Lewis*

In the book of Psalm, we are taught that the heavens are a declaration of God's glory. May we never cease to praise the Father for a universe that stands as an awesome testimony to His presence, to His power, and to His love.

A LESSON TO THINK ABOUT

God has given you everything. You must honor Him with your words, your actions, and your prayers.

What God's Word Says About Respecting God

Honor all people. Love the brotherhood. Fear God. Honor the king.

1 Peter 2:17 NKJV

Fear the Lord your God, serve him only and take your oaths in his name.

Deuteronomy 6:13 NIV

The fear of the Lord is the beginning of knowledge, but fools despise wisdom and discipline.

Proverbs 1:7 NIV

The fear of the Lord is a fountain of life . . . .

Proverbs 14:27 NIV

How blessed is everyone who fears the Lord, who walks in His ways.

Psalm 128:1 NASB

WORDS OF WISDOM ABOUT
THE CREATOR

The greatness of His power to create and design and form
and mold and make and build and arrange defies the limits
of our imagination. And since He created everything, there
is nothing beyond His power to fix or mend or heal or
restore.

Anne Graham Lotz

God is the beyond in the midst of our life.

Dietrich Bonhoeffer

God's actual divine essence and his will are absolutely
beyond all human thought, human understanding
or wisdom; in short, they are and ever will be
incomprehensible, inscrutable, and altogether hidden to
human reason.

Martin Luther

An infinite God can give all of Himself to each of His
children. He does not distribute Himself that each may have
a part, but to each one He gives all of Himself as fully as if
there were no others.

A. W. Tozer

Notes to Yourself: _____

_____

_____

_____

_____

_____

_____

_____

_____

_____

_____

_____

_____

As you consider the things you've written in the space above, ask yourself these questions:

Am I willing to put God first in my life?

Am I willing to honor Him with my talents, my time, and my testimony?

Do I praise God many times each day for His blessings and for His love?

PRAISE
THE LORD

*My soul, praise the Lord, and all that is within me,
praise His holy name. My soul, praise the Lord,
and do not forget all His benefits.*

Psalm 103:1-2 Holman CSB

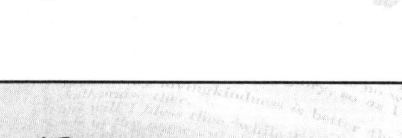

The Message

David praised the Lord with every fiber of his being.
Why? Because David was mindful of God's blessings.

When is the best time to praise God? In church? Before dinner is served? When we tuck little children into bed? None of the above. The best time to praise God is all day, every day, to the greatest extent we can, with thanksgiving in our hearts, and with a song on our lips.

Too many of us, even well-intentioned believers, tend to "compartmentalize" our waking hours into a few familiar categories: work, rest, play, family time, and worship. To do so is a mistake. Worship and praise should be woven into the fabric of everything we do; it should never be relegated to a weekly three-hour visit to church on Sunday morning.

> *Is anyone happy?*
> *Let him sing*
> *songs of praise.*
> James 5:13 NIV

The words by Fanny Crosby are familiar: "This is my story, this is my song, praising my Savior, all the day long." As believers who have been saved by the sacrifice of a risen Christ, we must do exactly as the song instructs: We must praise our Savior time and time again throughout the day. Worship and praise should be a part of everything we do. Otherwise, we quickly lose perspective as we fall prey to the demands of everyday life.

Theologian Wayne Oates once admitted, "Many of my prayers are made with my eyes open. You see, it seems I'm always praying about something, and it's not always convenient—or safe—to close my eyes." Dr. Oates understood that God always hears our prayers and that the relative position of our eyelids is of no concern to Him.

Do you sincerely desire to be a worthy servant of the One who has given you eternal love and eternal life? Then praise Him for who He is and for what He has done for you. And don't just praise Him on Sunday morning. Praise Him all day long, every day, for as long as you live . . . and then for all eternity.

A LESSON TO THINK ABOUT

God deserves your praise . . . and you deserve the experience of praising Him.

WHAT GOD'S WORD SAYS ABOUT PRAISE

Through Him then, let us continually offer up a sacrifice of praise to God, that is, the fruit of lips that give thanks to His name.

Hebrews 13:15 NASB

The LORD is my strength and song, and He has become my salvation; He is my God, and I will praise Him.

Exodus 15:2 NIV

And suddenly there was with the angel a multitude of the heavenly host praising God and saying: "Glory to God in the highest, And on earth peace, goodwill toward men!"

Luke 2:13-14 NKJV

At the name of Jesus every knee should bow, of those in heaven, and of those on earth, and of those under the earth, and that every tongue should confess that Jesus Christ is Lord, to the glory of God the Father.

Philippians 2:10-11 NKJV

WORDS OF WISDOM ABOUT
PRAISE

Praise and thank God for who He is and for what He has done for you.

Billy Graham

The joy of the Holy Spirit is experienced by giving thanks in all situations.

Bill Bright

It is always possible to be thankful for what is given rather than to complain about what is not given. One or the other becomes a habit of life.

Elisabeth Elliot

The act of thanksgiving is a demonstration of the fact that you are going to trust and believe God.

Kay Arthur

God is worthy of our praise and is pleased when we come before Him with thanksgiving.

Shirley Dobson

Notes to Yourself: _____

_____

_____

_____

_____

_____

_____

_____

_____

_____

_____

_____

As you consider the things you've written in the space above, ask yourself these questions:

Do I make it a habit to praise God many times each day, beginning with my morning devotional?

Whether I am experiencing good times or difficult times, do I understand the need to praise God?

Do I unfailingly praise God for His love, for His protection, for His blessings, and for His Son?

GOD FULFILLS
HIS PROMISES

As for God, his way is perfect.
All the LORD's promises prove true.
He is a shield for all who look to him for protection.

Psalm 18:30 NLT

The Message

David trusted God's promises. So must we.

In the 18th Psalm, David teaches us that God is trustworthy. Simply put, when God makes a promise, He keeps it.

God's promises are found in a book like no other: the Holy Bible. The Bible is a roadmap for life here on earth and for life eternal. As Christians, we are called upon to trust its promises, to follow its commandments, and to share its Good News.

If we wish to be faithful disciples of Christ, we must study the Bible daily and meditate upon its meaning for our lives. Otherwise, we deprive ourselves of a priceless gift from our Creator. God's Holy Word is, indeed, a transforming, life-changing, one-of-a-kind treasure. And, a passing acquaintance with the Good Book is insufficient for Christians who seek to obey God's Word and to understand His will.

> I need the spiritual revival that comes from spending quiet time alone with Jesus in prayer and in thoughtful meditation on His Word.
>
> *Anne Graham Lotz*

Is God's Word a lamp that guides your path? Is God's Word your indispensable compass for everyday living, or is it relegated to Sunday morning services? Do you read the Bible faithfully or sporadically? The answer to these questions will determine the direction of your thoughts, the direction of your day, and the direction of your life.

God's Word can be a roadmap to a place of righteousness and abundance. Make it your roadmap. God's wisdom can be a light to guide your steps. Claim it as your light today, tomorrow, and every day of your life—and then walk confidently in the footsteps of God's only begotten Son.

A LESSON TO THINK ABOUT

In your bookshelf you have God's roadmap for life here on earth and for life eternal. How you choose to use your Bible is, of course, up to you . . . and so are the consequences.

WHAT GOD'S WORD SAYS ABOUT GOD'S WORD

Heaven and earth will pass away, but My words will never pass away.

Matthew 24:35 Holman CSB

But the word of the Lord endures forever. And this is the word that was preached as the gospel to you.

1 Peter 1:25 Holman CSB

All Scripture is inspired by God and is profitable for teaching, for rebuking, for correcting, for training in righteousness, so that the man of God may be complete, equipped for every good work.

2 Timothy 3:16-17 Holman CSB

For the word of God is living and effective and sharper than any two-edged sword, penetrating as far as to divide soul, spirit, joints, and marrow; it is a judge of the ideas and thoughts of the heart.

Hebrews 4:12 Holman CSB

The one who is from God listens to God's words. This is why you don't listen, because you are not from God.

John 8:47 Holman CSB

WORDS OF WISDOM ABOUT
GOD'S WORD

Weave the unveiling fabric of God's word through your heart and mind. It will hold strong, even if the rest of life unravels.

Gigi Graham Tchividjian

God can see clearly no matter how dark or foggy the night is. Trust His Word to guide you safely home.

Lisa Whelchel

Words fail to express my love for this holy Book, my gratitude for its author, for His love and goodness. How shall I thank him for it?

Lottie Moon

The Bible became a living book and a guide for my life.

Vonette Bright

Notes to Yourself: _____

_____

_____

_____

_____

_____

_____

_____

_____

_____

_____

_____

_____

As you consider the things you've written in the space above, ask yourself these questions:

Do I make it a priority to read the Bible every day?

Do I consider regular Bible study to be an important source of wisdom?

Do I have a systematic plan for studying God's Word?

BE COMPASSIONATE; STRENGTHEN YOUR FELLOWSHIP

Behold, how good and how pleasant it is for brethren to dwell together in unity!

Psalm 133:1 NKJV

The Message

David praised the benefits of compassion, and he emphasized the need for fellowship.

David understood the need for believers to live together in unity. He knew that when likeminded believers worship together and work together, great things happen. But the opposite is also true: when church members begin to bicker—or when believers start to battle—Old Man Trouble is never far from the scene.

Anger is a natural human emotion that is sometimes necessary and appropriate. Even Jesus became angry when confronted with the moneychangers in the temple. Righteous indignation is an appropriate response to evil, but God does not intend that anger should rule our lives or our churches. Far from it. God intends that we turn away from anger whenever possible and forgive our neighbors as quickly as we can find it in our hearts to do so. When we do, compassion fills our hearts and our churches.

> *And let us be concerned about one another in order to promote love and good works.*
>
> *Hebrews 10:24 Holman CSB*

Your association with fellow Christians should be uplifting, enlightening, encouraging, and consistent. And make no mistake—if you genuinely want to build a closer relationship with God, you need to build closer relationships with godly people. That's why fellowship with upstanding men and women should be an integral part of your life.

Are you a builder of bridges inside your fellowship and throughout your community? If so, you can be sure that God will smile upon your endeavors. And you can be sure that He will bless you—and your fellowship—in surprising, miraculous ways. So make yourself this promise: vow to make a positive contribution to your church and to your world. It's the right thing to do and the right way to worship.

A LESSON TO THINK ABOUT

Compassionate words and deeds have echoes that last a lifetime and beyond.

WHAT GOD'S WORD SAYS ABOUT COMPASSION

I pray that your love for each other will overflow more and more, and that you will keep on growing in your knowledge and understanding.

Philippians 1:9 NLT

Finally, all of you be of one mind, having compassion for one another; love as brothers, be tenderhearted, be courteous.

1 Peter 3:8 NKJV

Therefore, God's chosen ones, holy and loved, put on heartfelt compassion, kindness, humility, gentleness, and patience.

Colossians 3:12 Holman CSB

But he's already made it plain how to live, what to do, what God is looking for in men and women. It's quite simple: Do what is fair and just to your neighbor, be compassionate and loyal in your love, and don't take yourself too seriously—take God seriously.

Micah 6:8 MSG

WORDS OF WISDOM ABOUT COMPASSION

The mark of a Christian is that he will walk the second mile and turn the other cheek. A wise man or woman gives the extra effort, all for the glory of the Lord Jesus Christ.

John Maxwell

When action-oriented compassion is absent, it's a tell-tale sign that something's spiritually amiss.

Bill Hybels

When you extend hospitality to others, you're not trying to impress people, you're trying to reflect God to them.

Max Lucado

Our Lord worked with people as they were, and He was patient—not tolerant of sin, but compassionate.

Vance Havner

Notes to Yourself: _____

_____

_____

_____

_____

_____

_____

_____

_____

_____

_____

_____

_____

As you consider the things you've written in the space above, ask yourself these questions:

Do I sometimes allow myself to become so busy that I fail to observe the needs of my friends and family?

As a Christian, am I willing to apply the Golden Rule in every situation?

When I perform an act of kindness, do I avoid public acclaim?

BE GRATEFUL, AND GIVE THANKS

I will give thanks to the LORD with all my heart;
I will tell of all Your wonders. I will be glad and exult in You;
I will sing praise to Your name, O Most High.

Psalm 9:1-2 NASB

The Message

David was thankful for God's blessings. We, too, must be quick to count our gifts and just as quick to thank the Giver.

D avid understood the importance of giving thanks to God, and so should you. So here's a question: If you sat down and began counting your blessings, how long would it take? If you answered, "A very long time," you're right. Your blessings include life, freedom, family, friends, talents, and possessions, for starters. But, your greatest blessing—a gift that is yours for the asking—is God's gift of salvation through Christ Jesus.

> The ability to rejoice
> in any situation
> is a sign of
> spiritual maturity.
>
> *Billy Graham*

God has blessed all of us beyond measure, and we owe Him everything, including our constant praise. That's why thanksgiving should become a habit, a regular part of our daily routines. When we slow down and express our gratitude to the One who made us, we enrich our own lives and the lives of those around us.

Dietrich Bonhoeffer observed, "It is only with gratitude that life becomes rich." These words most certainly apply to you.

Are you a thankful person? Do you appreciate the gifts that God has given you? And, do you demonstrate your gratitude by being a faithful steward of the gifts and talents that you have received from your Creator? You most certainly should be thankful. After all, when you stop to think about it, God has given you more gifts than you can count. So the question of the day is this: will you thank your Heavenly Father . . . or will you spend your time and energy doing other things?

God is always listening—are you willing to say thanks? It's up to you, and the next move is yours.

A LESSON TO THINK ABOUT

By speaking words of thanksgiving and praise, you honor the Father and you protect your heart against the twin evils of apathy and ingratitude.

WHAT GOD'S WORD SAYS ABOUT THANKSGIVING

Thanks be to God for His indescribable gift.

2 Corinthians 9:15 Holman CSB

And let the peace of the Messiah, to which you were also called in one body, control your hearts. Be thankful.

Colossians 3:15 Holman CSB

Therefore as you have received Christ Jesus the Lord, walk in Him, rooted and built up in Him and established in the faith, just as you were taught, and overflowing with thankfulness.

Colossians 2:6-7 Holman CSB

It is good to give thanks to the Lord, And to sing praises to Your name, O Most High.

Psalm 92:1 NKJV

Enter into His gates with thanksgiving, and into His courts with praise. Be thankful to Him, and bless His name. For the Lord is good; His mercy is everlasting, and His truth endures to all generations.

Psalm 100:4-5 NKJV

WORDS OF WISDOM ABOUT THANKSGIVING

The act of thanksgiving is a demonstration of the fact that you are going to trust and believe God.

Kay Arthur

Thanksgiving is good but Thanksliving is better.

Jim Gallery

Thanksgiving or complaining—these words express two contrastive attitudes of the souls of God's children in regard to His dealings with them. The soul that gives thanks can find comfort in everything; the soul that complains can find comfort in nothing.

Hannah Whitall Smith

A child of God should be a visible beatitude for joy and a living doxology for gratitude.

C. H. Spurgeon

Notes to Yourself: _____

_____

_____

_____

_____

_____

_____

_____

_____

_____

_____

_____

_____

As you consider the things you've written in the space above, ask yourself these questions:

Am I determined not to take my blessings for granted?

Will I remain humble as I praise God and thank Him for His gifts?

Will I treasure my talents and use them to honor God?

LESSON 25

WORSHIP GOD

Give unto the Lord, O you mighty ones,
give unto the Lord glory and strength. Give unto the Lord
the glory due to His name; worship the Lord in the beauty of
holiness. The voice of the Lord is over the waters;
the God of glory thunders; The Lord is over many waters.

Psalm 29:1-3 NKJV

The Message

David's instructions were clear: we should worship God
with praise on our lips and righteousness in our hearts.

All of humanity is engaged in worship. The question is not whether we worship, but what we worship. Wise men and women choose to worship God. When they do, they are blessed with a plentiful harvest of joy, peace, and abundance. Other people choose to distance themselves from God by foolishly worshiping things that are intended to bring personal gratification but not spiritual gratification. Such choices often have tragic consequences.

If we place our love for material possessions above our love for God—or if we yield to the countless temptations of this world—we find ourselves engaged in a struggle between good and evil, a clash between God and Satan. Our responses to these struggles have implications that echo throughout our families and throughout our communities.

> Worship is a daunting task. Each worships differently. But each should worship.
>
> *Max Lucado*

How can we ensure that we cast our lot with God? We do so, in part, by the practice of regular, purposeful worship in the company of fellow believers. When we worship God faithfully and fervently, we are blessed. When we fail to worship God, for whatever reason, we forfeit the spiritual gifts that He intends for us.

We must worship our Heavenly Father, not just with our words, but also with deeds. We must honor Him, praise Him, and obey Him. As we seek to find purpose and meaning for our lives, we must first seek His purpose and His will. For believers, God comes first. Always first.

Do you place a high value on the practice of worship? Hopefully so. After all, every day provides countless opportunities to put God where He belongs: at the very center of your life. It's up to you to worship God seven days a week; anything less is simply not enough.

A LESSON TO THINK ABOUT

When you worship God with a sincere heart, He will guide your steps and bless your life.

WHAT GOD'S WORD SAYS ABOUT WORSHIP

But the hour cometh, and now is, when the true worshippers shall worship the Father in spirit and in truth: for the Father seeketh such to worship him.

John 4:23 KJV

Then saith Jesus unto him, Get thee hence, Satan: for it is written, Thou shalt worship the Lord thy God, and him only shalt thou serve.

Matthew 4:10 KJV

Blessed are they which do hunger and thirst after righteousness: for they shall be filled.

Matthew 5:6 KJV

Worship the Lord with gladness. Come before him, singing with joy. Acknowledge that the Lord is God! He made us, and we are his. We are his people, the sheep of his pasture.

Psalm 100:2-3 NLT

Happy are those who hear the joyful call to worship, for they will walk in the light of your presence, Lord.

Psalm 89:15 NLT

WORDS OF WISDOM ABOUT
WORSHIP

Each time, before you intercede, be quiet first and worship God in His glory. Think of what He can do and how He delights to hear the prayers of His redeemed people. Think of your place and privilege in Christ, and expect great things!

Andrew Murray

Worship is spiritual. Our worship must be more than just outward expression, it must also take place in our spirits.

Franklin Graham

Inside the human heart is an undeniable, spiritual instinct to commune with its Creator.

Jim Cymbala

Worship is not taught from the pulpit. It must be learned in the heart.

Jim Elliot

Notes to Yourself: _____

_____

_____

_____

_____

_____

_____

_____

_____

_____

_____

_____

_____

As you consider the things you've written in the space above, ask yourself these questions:

Do I believe that it is important to worship God every day of the week, not just on Sundays?

Do I feel that it is important to worship regularly with a community of believers?

Do I have a quiet place where I can go, a place where God seems especially close?

GOD OFFERS JOY

You will show me the path of life;
in Your presence is fullness of joy;
at Your right hand are pleasures forevermore.

Psalm 16:11 NKJV

The Message

David understood that true fulfillment comes whenever we live in accordance with God's laws. God has a plan for each of us, and when we live in accordance with His plan, we experience abundance and joy.

David understood that lasting joy comes from God . . . and you should understand it, too. Do you seek happiness, abundance, and contentment? If so, here are some things you should do: Love God and His Son; depend upon God for strength; try, to the best of your abilities, to follow God's will; and strive to obey His Holy Word. When you do these things, you'll discover that happiness goes hand-in-hand with righteousness. The happiest people are not those who rebel against God; the happiest people are those who love God and obey His commandments.

> Joy is the heart's harmonious response to the Lord's song of love.
>
> *A. W. Tozer*

Psalm 100 reminds us that, as believers, we have every reason to celebrate: "Shout for joy to the LORD, all the earth. Worship the LORD with gladness" (vv. 1-2 NIV). Yet sometimes, amid the inevitable hustle and bustle of life here on earth, we can forfeit—albeit temporarily—the joy that God intends for our lives.

C. H. Spurgeon, the renowned 19th-century English clergyman, advised, "Rejoicing is clearly a spiritual command. To ignore it, I need to remind you, is disobedience." As Christians, we are called by our Creator

---

to live abundantly, prayerfully, and joyfully. To do otherwise is to squander His spiritual gifts.

What does life have in store for you? A world full of possibilities (of course it's up to you to seize them) and God's promise of abundance (of course it's up to you to accept it). So, as you embark upon the next phase of your journey, remember to celebrate the life that God has given you. Your Creator has blessed you beyond measure. Honor Him with your prayers, your words, your deeds, and your joy.

A LESSON TO THINK ABOUT

Joy does not depend upon your circumstances; it depends upon your thoughts and upon your relationship with God.

WHAT GOD'S WORD SAYS ABOUT JOY

I have spoken these things to you so that My joy may be in you and your joy may be complete.

John 15:11 Holman CSB

Rejoice in the Lord always. I will say it again: Rejoice!

Philippians 4:4 Holman CSB

Delight yourself also in the Lord, and He shall give you the desires of your heart.

Psalm 37:4 NKJV

Make me hear joy and gladness.

Psalm 51:8 NKJV

Weeping may spend the night, but there is joy in the morning.

Psalm 30:5 Holman CSB

WORDS OF WISDOM ABOUT JOY

Our God is so wonderfully good, and lovely, and blessed in every way that the mere fact of belonging to Him is enough for an untellable fullness of joy!

Hannah Whitall Smith

Joy is the direct result of having God's perspective on our daily lives and the effect of loving our Lord enough to obey His commands and trust His promises.

Bill Bright

Our sense of joy, satisfaction, and fulfillment in life increases, no matter what the circumstances, if we are in the center of God's will.

Billy Graham

If you can forgive the person you were, accept the person you are, and believe in the person you will become, you are headed for joy. So celebrate your life.

Barbara Johnson

Notes to Yourself: _____

_____

_____

_____

_____

_____

_____

_____

_____

_____

_____

_____

_____

As you consider the things you've written in the space above, ask yourself these questions:

Do I try to treat each day as a cause for celebration?

Do I praise God many times each day?

Am I willing to share my enthusiasm with family, with friends, and with the world?

PLEASE GOD FIRST

Let the words of my mouth and the meditation
of my heart be acceptable in Your sight, O Lord,
my strength and my Redeemer.

Psalm 19:14 NKJV

The Message

David knew that his first obligation was to please God, not men. And David also understood that by pleasing God, David would avail himself of God's power.

D avid knew the importance of pleasing God first. It's a lesson that all of us should learn, yet far too many of us invest too much energy trying to meet society's expectations and too little energy trying to please the Creator. It's a common behavior, but it's also a very big mistake.

A better strategy, of course, is to try to please God first. To do so, you must prioritize your day according to God's commandments, and you must seek His will and His wisdom in all matters. Then, you can face each day with the assurance that the same God who created our universe out of nothingness will help you place first things first in your own life.

> If you love Me,
> you will keep
> My commandments.
> John 14:15 Holman CSB

When God made you, He equipped you with an array of talents and abilities that are uniquely yours. It's up to you to discover those talents and to use them, but sometimes the world will encourage you to do otherwise. At times, society will attempt to cubbyhole you, to standardize you, and to make you fit into a particular, preformed mold. Perhaps God has other plans.

Sometimes, because you're an imperfect human being, you may become so wrapped up in meeting society's expectations that you fail to focus on God's expectations. To do so is a mistake of major proportions—don't make it. Instead, seek God's guidance as you focus your energies on becoming the person God wants you to be.

Are you having trouble choosing between God's priorities and society's priorities? Are you feeling overwhelmed or confused? If so, turn the concerns over to God—prayerfully, earnestly, and often. Then, listen for His answer . . . and trust the answer He gives.

A LESSON TO THINK ABOUT

You should be far more concerned with pleasing God than with pleasing any person on earth (including yourself).

WHAT GOD'S WORD SAYS ABOUT PLEASING GOD

Obviously, I'm not trying to be a people pleaser! No, I am trying to please God. If I were still trying to please people, I would not be Christ's servant.

Galatians 1:10 NLT

Be energetic in your life of salvation, reverent and sensitive before God. That energy is God's energy, an energy deep within you, God himself willing and working at what will give him the most pleasure.

Philippians 2:12-13 MSG

Everything that goes into a life of pleasing God has been miraculously given to us by getting to know, personally and intimately, the One who invited us to God. The best invitation we ever received!

2 Peter 1:3 MSG

Our only goal is to please God whether we live here or there, because we must all stand before Christ to be judged.

2 Corinthians 5:9-10 NCV

Words of Wisdom About
Pleasing God

Make God's will the focus of your life day by day. If you seek to please Him and Him alone, you'll find yourself satisfied with life.

Kay Arthur

Every Christian would agree that a man's spiritual health is exactly proportional to his love for God.

C. S. Lewis

It takes faith to obey God, but God always rewards obedient faith.

Warren Wiersbe

Faithfulness today is the best preparation for the demands of tomorrow.

Elisabeth Elliot

You must never sacrifice your relationship with God for the sake of a relationship with another person.

Charles Stanley

Notes to Yourself: _____

_____

_____

_____

_____

_____

_____

_____

_____

_____

_____

_____

_____

As you consider the things you've written in the space above, ask yourself these questions:

Do I understand the importance of pleasing God first and people later, or am I sometimes too focused on pleasing people?

Do I try to associate with people who, by their actions and their words, encourage me to become a better person?

Do I understand that it's more important to be respected than to be liked?

STRIVE FOR HOLINESS

Who may ascend into the hill of the Lord? Or who may
stand in His holy place? He who has clean hands and a pure
heart, who has not lifted up his soul to an idol, nor sworn
deceitfully. He shall receive blessing from the Lord,
and righteousness from the God of his salvation.

Psalm 24:3-5 NKJV

The Message

David instructs us that in order to occupy God's holy
place, we should endeavor to make ourselves holy.
Obedience to God is another form of worship.

David understood that life is a series of choices. Each day, we make countless decisions that can bring us closer to God . . . or not. When we live according to God's commandments—when we lead holy lives that honor the Creator—we earn for ourselves the abundance and peace that He intends for us to experience. But, when we turn our backs upon God by ignoring Him—or by disobeying Him—we bring needless pain and suffering upon ourselves and our families.

Oswald Chambers, the author of the Christian classic devotional text, *My Utmost for His Highest*, advised, "Never support an experience which does not have God as its source, and faith in God as its result." These words serve as a powerful reminder that, as Christians, we are called to walk with God and obey His commandments. But, we live in a world that presents us with countless temptations to stray far from God's path.

> No Christian can have a sacred ambition for holiness which the Lord is not prepared to fulfill.
>
> C. H. *Spurgeon*

We Christians, when confronted with sin, have clear instructions: Walk—or better yet run— in the opposite direction.

Do you want God's peace and His blessings? Then obey Him. When you're faced with a difficult choice or a powerful temptation, seek God's counsel and trust the counsel He gives. Invite God into your heart and live according to His commandments. And when God speaks to you through that little quiet voice that He has placed in your heart, listen. When you do, you will be blessed today and tomorrow and forever. And you'll discover that happiness means living in accordance with your beliefs. No exceptions.

A LESSON TO THINK ABOUT

God is holy and wants you to be holy. You should make certain that your response to God's love is obedience to Him.

WHAT GOD'S WORD SAYS ABOUT HOLINESS

Real wisdom, God's wisdom, begins with a holy life and is characterized by getting along with others. It is gentle and reasonable, overflowing with mercy and blessings, not hot one day and cold the next, not two-faced.

James 3:17 MSG

Pursue peace with all people, and holiness, without which no one will see the Lord.

Hebrews 12:14 NKJV

Since everything here today might well be gone tomorrow, do you see how essential it is to live a holy life?

2 Peter 3:11 MSG

But now you must be holy in everything you do, just as God—who chose you to be his children—is holy. For he himself has said, "You must be holy because I am holy."

1 Peter 1:15-16 NLT

You will teach me how to live a holy life. Being with you will fill me with joy; at your right hand I will find pleasure forever.

Psalm 16:11 NCV

WORDS OF WISDOM ABOUT HOLINESS

Holiness is not an impossibility for any of us.

Elisabeth Elliot

Holiness isn't in a style of dress. It's not a matter of rules and regulations. It's a way of life that emanates quietness and rest, joy in family, shared pleasures with friends, the help of a neighbor—and the hope of a Savior.

Joni Eareckson Tada

The destined end of man is not happiness, nor health, but holiness. God's one aim is the production of saints. He is not an eternal blessing machine for men; he did not come to save men out of pity; he came to save men because he had created them to be holy.

Oswald Chambers

Holiness should be a constant goal for all of us. Christ prepares us for the perfection of heaven by lessening the imperfections of earth.

Shirley Dobson

Notes to Yourself: _____

_____

_____

_____

_____

_____

_____

_____

_____

_____

_____

_____

As you consider the things you've written in the space above, ask yourself these questions:

Do I place a high value on worshipping God and obeying Him?

Do I believe that, with God's help, I can be a holy person?

When faced with an important decision, am I willing to pray about it before I decide, not after?

GOD IS THE SOURCE OF WISDOM

Show me thy ways, O LORD; teach me thy paths.
Lead me in thy truth, and teach me:
for thou art the God of my salvation;
on thee do I wait all the day.

Psalm 25:4-5 KJV

The Message

David asked God for wisdom, and so should we. God's wisdom is the ultimate wisdom.

Where can we find wisdom? David understood that real wisdom begins and ends with God. Do you understand it, too? If so you will be blessed. Proverbs 1:7 instructs us that "Knowledge begins with respect for the Lord, but fools hate wisdom and self-control" (NCV). And intuitively, we know those words to be true—yet all too often, we fail to live by them. Instead of honoring God by placing Him first in our lives, we become preoccupied with the countless demands of our complicated world. When we allow our thoughts and emotions to be hijacked by the inevitable distractions that accompany life here on earth, we distance ourselves from the only wisdom that really matters: God's wisdom.

> Wisdom is the God-given ability to see life with rare objectivity and to handle life with rare stability.
>
> *Charles Swindoll*

In theory, all of us would like to be wise, but not all of us are willing to do the work that is required to become wise. Wisdom is not like a mushroom; it does not spring up overnight. It is, instead, like an oak tree that starts as a tiny acorn, grows into a sapling, and eventually reaches up to the sky, tall and strong.

To become wise, we must seek God's wisdom and live according to His Word. To become wise, we must seek wisdom with consistency and purpose. To become wise, we must not only learn the lessons of the Christian life, we must also live by them.

Do you seek to live a life of righteousness and wisdom? If so, you must study the ultimate source of wisdom: the Word of God. You must seek out worthy mentors and listen carefully to their advice. You must associate, day in and day out, with godly men and women. Then, as you accumulate wisdom, you must not keep it for yourself; you must, instead, share it with your friends and family members. But be forewarned: if you sincerely seek to share your hard-earned wisdom with others, your actions must give credence to your words. The best way to share one's wisdom—perhaps the only way—is not by words, but by example.

A LESSON TO THINK ABOUT

God makes His wisdom available to you. Your job is to acknowledge, to understand, and (above all) to use that wisdom.

WHAT GOD'S WORD SAYS ABOUT WISDOM

Therefore, everyone who hears these words of Mine and acts on them will be like a sensible man who built his house on the rock. The rain fell, the rivers rose, and the winds blew and pounded that house. Yet it didn't collapse, because its foundation was on the rock.

Matthew 7:24–25 Holman CSB

But from Him you are in Christ Jesus, who for us became wisdom from God, as well as righteousness, sanctification, and redemption.

1 Corinthians 1:30 Holman CSB

For God has not given us a spirit of fearfulness, but one of power, love, and sound judgment.

2 Timothy 1:7 Holman CSB

Now if any of you lacks wisdom, he should ask God, who gives to all generously and without criticizing, and it will be given to him.

James 1:5 Holman CSB

WORDS OF WISDOM ABOUT WISDOM

Having a doctrine pass before the mind is not what the Bible means by knowing the truth. It's only when it reaches down deep into the heart that the truth begins to set us free, just as a key must penetrate a lock to turn it, or as rainfall must saturate the earth down to the roots in order for your garden to grow.

John Eldredge

The fruit of wisdom is Christlikeness, peace, humility, and love. And, the root of it is faith in Christ as the manifested wisdom of God.

J. I. Packer

This is my song through endless ages: Jesus led me all the way.

Fanny Crosby

The essence of wisdom, from a practical standpoint, is pausing long enough to look at our lives—invitations, opportunities, relationships—from God's perspective. And then acting on it.

Charles Stanley

Notes to Yourself: _____

_____

_____

_____

_____

_____

_____

_____

_____

_____

_____

_____

_____

As you consider the things you've written in the space above, ask yourself these questions:

Do I continually remind myself of God's wisdom by reading the Bible each day?

Will I do my best to live wisely by obeying the teachings that I find in God's Word?

Will I associate with wise men and wise women?

YOU ARE FORGIVEN . . . YOU SHOULD BE FORGIVING

*Blessed is he whose transgression is forgiven,
whose sin is covered. Blessed is the man to whom
the Lord does not impute iniquity,
and in whose spirit there is no deceit.*

Psalm 32:1-2 NKJV

The Message

When we ask God for His forgiveness, He gives it. And because we are blessed by God's gift of forgiveness, we should be willing—indeed anxious—to forgive others.

From firsthand experience, David understood that God forgives sin. You should understand it, too. The Bible promises you this: When you ask God for forgiveness, He will give it. No questions asked; no explanations required.

God's power to forgive, like His love, is infinite. Despite your shortcomings, despite your sins, God offers you immediate forgiveness. It's time to take Him up on His offer.

When it comes to forgiveness, God doesn't play favorites and neither should you. You should forgive all the people who have harmed you (not just the people who have asked for forgiveness or the ones who have made restitution). Complete forgiveness is God's way, and it should be your way, too. Anything less is not enough.

> *Blessed are the merciful, because they will be shown mercy.*
>
> Matthew 5:7 Holman CSB

Life would be much simpler if we could forgive people "once and for all" and be done with it. But forgiveness is seldom that easy. For most of us, the decision to forgive is straightforward, but the process of forgiving is more difficult. Forgiveness is a journey that requires effort, time, perseverance, and prayer.

Today, as you go about your daily affairs, remember that you have already been forgiven by your Heavenly Father, and so, too, should you forgive others. If you bear bitterness against anyone, take your bitterness to God and leave it there. If you are angry, pray for God's healing hand to calm your spirit. If you are troubled by some past injustice, read God's Word and remember His commandment to forgive. When you follow that commandment and sincerely forgive those who have hurt you, you'll discover that a heavy burden has been lifted from your shoulders. And, you'll discover that although forgiveness is indeed difficult, with God's help, all things are possible.

A LESSON TO THINK ABOUT

Forgiveness is its own reward. Bitterness is its own punishment. Guard your words and your thoughts accordingly.

WHAT GOD'S WORD SAYS ABOUT FORGIVENESS

Be merciful, just as your Father also is merciful.

Luke 6:36 Holman CSB

All bitterness, anger and wrath, insult and slander must be removed from you, along with all wickedness. And be kind and compassionate to one another, forgiving one another, just as God also forgave you in Christ.

Ephesians 4:31-32 Holman CSB

Then Peter came to Him and said, "Lord, how many times could my brother sin against me and I forgive him? As many as seven times?" "I tell you, not as many as seven," Jesus said to him, "but 70 times seven."

Matthew 18:21-22 Holman CSB

You have heard that it was said, You shall love your neighbor and hate your enemy. But I tell you, love your enemies, and pray for those who persecute you, so that you may be sons of your Father in heaven.

Matthew 5:43-45 Holman CSB

WORDS OF WISDOM ABOUT
FORGIVENESS

Forgiveness is actually the best revenge because it not only sets us free from the person we forgive, but it frees us to move into all that God has in store for us.

Stormie Omartian

We are products of our past, but we don't have to be prisoners of it. God specializes in giving people a fresh start.

Rick Warren

Miracles broke the physical laws of the universe; forgiveness broke the moral rules.

Philip Yancey

Bitterness is the trap that snares the hunter.

Max Lucado

Forgiveness is contagious. First you forgive them, and pretty soon, they'll forgive you, too.

Marie T. Freeman

Notes to Yourself: _____

_____

_____

_____

_____

_____

_____

_____

_____

_____

_____

_____

_____

As you consider the things you've written in the space above, ask yourself these questions:

Am I willing to acknowledge the important role that forgiveness should play in my life?

Will I strive to forgive those who have hurt me, even when doing so is difficult?

Do I understand that forgiveness is a marathon (not a sprint), and will I prayerfully ask God to help me move beyond the emotions of bitterness and regret?

SELECTED BIBLE VERSES AUTHORED BY DAVID

ARRANGED BY TOPIC

ADVERSITY

May the Lord answer you when you are in distress; may the name of the God of Jacob protect you.

Psalm 20:1 NIV

He restoreth my soul: he leadeth me in the paths of righteousness for his name's sake.

Psalm 23:3 KJV

Blessed be the LORD, because he hath heard the voice of my supplications. The LORD is my strength and my shield; my heart trusted in him, and I am helped . . . .

Psalm 28:6-7 KJV

CONTENTMENT

The LORD will give strength to His people; The LORD will bless His people with peace.

Psalm 29:11 NKJV

Because your love is better than life, my lips will glorify you. I will praise you as long as I live, and in your name I will lift up my hands. My soul will be satisfied as with the richest of foods; with singing lips my mouth will praise you.

Psalm 63:3-5 NIV

COURAGE

Be strong and courageous, all you who put your hope in the Lord.

Psalm 31:24 Holman CSB

I sought the LORD, and he answered me; he delivered me from all my fears.

Psalm 34:4 NIV

Even when I go through the darkest valley, I fear no danger, for You are with me.

Psalm 23:4 Holman CSB

ENVY

Do not fret because of evil men or be envious of those who do wrong . . . .

Psalm 37:1 NIV

Stop your anger! Turn from your rage! Do not envy others—it only leads to harm.

Psalm 37:8 NLT

Evil

I will set no wicked thing before mine eyes . . . .

Psalm 101:3 KJV

The face of the Lord is set against those who do what is evil.

Psalm 34:16 Holman CSB

Fret not thyself because of evildoers, neither be thou envious against the workers of iniquity. For they shall soon be cut down like the grass, and wither as the green herb.

Psalm 37:1-2 KJV

God judgeth the righteous, and God is angry with the wicked every day.

Psalm 7:11 KJV

Faith

Blessed are they that put their trust in him.

Psalm 2:12 KJV

Cast your burden on the Lord, And He shall sustain you; He shall never permit the righteous to be moved.

Psalm 55:22 NKJV

FEAR

I cried out to the Lord in my suffering, and he heard me. He set me free from all my fears.

Psalm 34:6 NLT

What time I am afraid, I will trust in thee.

Psalm 56:3 KJV

GOD'S BLESSINGS

Those who are blessed by Him will inherit the land.

Psalm 37:22 Holman CSB

My cup runs over. Surely goodness and mercy shall follow me all the days of my life; and I will dwell in the house of the Lord forever.

Psalm 23:5-6 NKJV

Victory comes from you, O Lord. May your blessings rest on your people.

Psalm 3:8 NLT

GOD'S CREATION

The heavens declare the glory of God, and the sky proclaims the work of His hands.

Psalm 19:1 Holman CSB

When I observe Your heavens, the work of Your fingers, the moon and the stars, which You set in place, what is man that You remember him?

Psalm 8:3-4 Holman CSB

GOD'S LOVE

But the love of the Lord remains forever with those who fear him. His salvation extends to the children's children of those who are faithful to his covenant, of those who obey his commandments!

Psalm 103:17-18 NLT

Help me, Lord my God; save me according to Your faithful love.

Psalm 109:26 Holman CSB

The LORD's unfailing love surrounds the man who trusts in him.

Psalm 32:10 NIV

GOD'S MERCY

But the mercy of the LORD is from everlasting to everlasting upon them that fear him, and his righteousness unto children's children . . . .

Psalm 103:17 KJV

The LORD is gracious and full of compassion, slow to anger and great in mercy. The LORD is good to all, and His tender mercies are over all His works.

Psalm 145:8-9 NKJV

GOD'S PLAN

The Lord will perfect that which concerns me; Your mercy, O Lord, endures forever.

Psalm 138:8 NKJV

O Lord, you have examined my heart and know everything about me. You know when I sit down or stand up. You know my every thought when far away. You chart the path ahead of me and tell me where to stop and rest.

Psalm 139:1-3 NLT

GOD'S POWER

For the kingdom is the LORD's: and his is the governor among the nations.

Psalm 22:28 KJV

Proclaim the power of God, whose majesty is over Israel, whose power is in the skies. You are awesome, O God, in your sanctuary; the God of Israel gives power and strength to his people. Praise be to God!

Psalm 68:34-35 NIV

GOD'S PRESENCE

The Lord is near all who call out to Him, all who call out to Him with integrity. He fulfills the desires of those who fear Him; He hears their cry for help and saves them.

Psalm 145:18-19 Holman CSB

I have set the Lord always before me; because He is at my right hand I shall not be moved.

Psalm 16:8 NKJV

Surely goodness and mercy shall follow me all the days of my life: and I will dwell in the house of the Lord for ever.

Psalm 23:6 KJV

GOD'S PROTECTION

Our help is in the name of the Lord, the Maker of heaven and earth.

Psalm 124:8 Holman CSB

The Lord is my rock, my fortress, and my deliverer.

Psalm 18:2 Holman CSB

For surely, O LORD, you bless the righteous; you surround them with your favor as with a shield.

Psalm 5:12 NIV

GOD'S SUPPORT

But thou, O LORD, art a shield for me . . . .

Psalm 3:3 KJV

Incline Your ear to me, rescue me quickly; Be to me a rock of strength, A stronghold to save me.

Psalm 31:2 NASB

The LORD is close to the brokenhearted and saves those who are crushed in spirit.

Psalm 34:18 NIV

Hope

Lord, I turn my hope to You. My God, I trust in You.

Psalm 25:1-2 Holman CSB

Those who hope in the LORD will inherit the land.

Psalm 37:9 NIV

For in thee, O LORD, do I hope: thou wilt hear, O Lord my God.

Psalm 38:15 KJV

He put a new song in my mouth, a hymn of praise to our God. Many will see and fear and put their trust in the LORD.

Psalm 40:3 NIV

Joy

Weeping may spend the night, but there is joy in the morning.

Psalm 30:5 Holman CSB

I will thank the Lord with all my heart; I will declare all Your wonderful works. I will rejoice and boast about You; I will sing about Your name, Most High.

Psalm 9:1-2 Holman CSB

Praise

I will praise You with my whole heart.

Psalm 138:1 NKJV

Every day will I bless thee; and I will praise thy name for ever and ever.

Psalm 145:2 KJV

Great is the Lord, and greatly to be praised; And His greatness is unsearchable.

Psalm 145:3 NKJV

I will praise the Lord at all times, I will constantly speak his praises.

Psalm 34:1 NLT

Prayer

In my distress I called upon the LORD; I cried unto my God for help. From his temple, he heard my voice.

Psalm 18:6 NIV

Therefore, let everyone who is godly pray to You.

Psalm 32:6 NASB

RENEWAL

He makes me to lie down in green pastures; He leads me beside the still waters. He restores my soul; He leads me in the paths of righteousness for His name's sake.

Psalm 23:2-3 NKJV

Create in me a pure heart, O God, and renew a steadfast spirit within me. Do not cast me from your presence or take your Holy Spirit from me. Restore to me the joy of your salvation and grant me a willing spirit, to sustain me.

Psalm 51:10-12 NIV

RIGHTEOUSNESS

The righteous face many troubles, but the Lord rescues them from each and every one.

Psalm 34:19 NLT

For the Lord is righteous, He loves righteousness; His countenance beholds the upright.

Psalm 11:7 NKJV

You can be sure of this: The Lord has set apart the godly for himself.

Psalm 4:3 NLT

TRUSTING GOD

In thee, O Lord, do I put my trust.

Psalm 31:1 KJV

Commit everything you do to the Lord. Trust him, and he will help you.

Psalm 37:5 NLT

In God have I put my trust: I will not be afraid what man can do unto me.

Psalm 56:11 KJV

My heart is steadfast, O God, my heart is steadfast.

Psalm 57:7 NASB

O Lord my God, in You I put my trust; save me from all those who persecute me; and deliver me . . . .

Psalm 7:1 NKJV

Those who know Your name trust in You because You have not abandoned those who seek You, Lord.

Psalm 9:10 Holman CSB